Revised Edition

# THE INDIGENOUS CHURCH

INCLUDING
The Indigenous Church *and the* Missionary

## MELVIN L. HODGES

*Foreword by* **L. John Bueno**

**GPH**®

Gospel Publishing House
Springfield, Missouri
02-0528

*The Indigenous Church* © 1953, 1971, 1976 by Gospel Publishing House, 1445 N. Boonville Ave., Springfield, MO 65802.

The original appendices from *The Indigenous Church* were not included in this edition. Because of its historical significance the appendices have been made available on the Flower Pentecostal Heritage Center's Web site:
http://www.ifphc.org/hodges

*The Indigenous Church and the Missionary* © 1978 by Melvin L. Hodges was published by the William Carey Library.

Both *The Indigenous Church* and *The Indigenous Church and the Missionary* have been significantly revised for the contemporary student of missionary indigenous principles. It is hoped that this new edition will make Melvin Hodges' important work accessible to these students.

ISBN 978-0-88243-810-8

Printed in United States of America

# Contents

# Foreword 2009

I had the privilege of working firsthand with Melvin Hodges, one of the great missionary heroes of the Assemblies of God. He was not only my regional director when I first went to the field, but he also became my friend. I was privileged to be with him in retreats and seminars and hear what was on his heart. Through these experiences, I sensed the great wisdom God had given him as it relates to the indigenous church. Over the years I saw the fruit of his efforts in the lives of those he mentored.

As a missionary to El Salvador, Brother Hodges first put the indigenous church concept into practice. While many of the principles he used were not original with him, he was the one who incorporated them in the real world. The leaders who came under his tutelage during this era were men I greatly admired when I was starting out as a missionary.

In those early years, missionaries and national pastors in El Salvador exemplified teamwork. They literally walked, ate, and slept with one goal in mind—to prepare workers who would extend the church to unreached areas. They were totally absorbed in their mission and poured into others the great virtues of Scripture and correct missiological thinking. They were great men in their own right and helped lead their nation into the strong church that developed over the years. Today some statistics claim that as much as 30 percent of El Salvador's population is born again.

To witness indigenous church principles lived out and developed down through the years has been a distinct thrill. When I served as regional director for Latin America and the Caribbean—a position Brother Hodges once occupied—I saw the influence these teachings had, not just in one country but throughout the entire region. In countries where the principles were accepted, the church showed great growth, strength, and leadership. In the places where believers tried to bypass their application, the church was weak and ineffective.

Laying a foundation in correlation with the three selfs of the indigenous church principles has required years of hard work and prayer. Yet now the benefit of such effort is clear. Latin America in many cases is an example of what can happen when these principles are put into place. While other factors undoubtedly contributed to the revival we see there today, I believe that the practice of indigenous church principles is a major factor in the development of strong churches throughout the region.

As executive director of World Missions, I have observed this same phenomenon worldwide. The influence of Brother Hodges and others, such as Morris Williams, former regional director for Africa, and the partnership principles he developed have confirmed the wisdom of the basic missiology of indigenization. Throughout the world, churches are developed and strong because of these basic principles, and their leaders are willing to take responsibility for their own people with an attitude of strength and maturity.

I will always treasure the moments I spent with Brother Hodges and the great leaders he trained in the early years of his ministry. I have seen the wisdom of his teaching and his devotion to the Master. He was a true servant of the Master and reflected a godly spirit in everything he did. He did more than talk about his relationship with God; he gave us an example to follow. Watching the fruit of his ministry made me a true believer in the indigenous church.

L. John Bueno
Executive Director
Assemblies of God World Missions

# Introduction 2009

Melvin Hodges' legacy and impact on missions is best understood in the context of Assemblies of God (AG) missions history and the task still before us.

After ninety-four years of AG missions, more than sixty million believers worship in more than three hundred thousand congregations in 212 countries and territories. But this represents just over 1 percent of the world's vast, unreached multitudes. When we consider the challenging task of reaching our world, how can we hope to see the Great Commission fulfilled?

In recent years the term *best practices* has become common. This term describes a management approach that seeks the most efficient and effective processes and methods to produce a desired outcome. Best practices, then, are based on repeatable procedures that have proved themselves over time.

Early AG missions leaders were committed to a *best-practices* approach long before the term came into popular use. In 1914, at the second General Council of the Assemblies of God, this resolution was made: "We commit ourselves and the Movement to Him for the greatest evangelism the world has ever seen." These words were not born out of fervent optimism or self-confidence, but a heartfelt, intentional response to the command of our Lord to go into *all* the world. It reflects both a comprehension and an apprehension of our Lord's promise concerning the Spirit's empowerment to accomplish the task.

Another resolution passed seven years later at the 1921 Council was even more significant in the history of our mission because it determined *how* we could fulfill the declaration made in 1914. It stipulated that we would guide our mission using *New Testament practices.* Among the six practices listed was the following: "It shall be our purpose to seek to establish self-supporting, self-propagating, and self-governing native churches."

What the resolution describes as "self-supporting, self-propagating, and self-governing 'native' churches" is now known by the term *indigenous churches. Indigenous* describes churches that begin, grow, and live in their own natural setting or environment. Our early leaders determined that the Fellowship's mission was not to transplant the American church but to establish a body of believers that would live and grow without being dependent on the U.S. church that sent the missionaries.

Melvin Hodges is one of several AG missionaries and leaders who were especially influential in establishing indigenous church principles and practices. The first, Alice Luce, was significantly influenced by Roland Allen, an Anglican missionary to China. During Allen's missionary work, he began to reevaluate missionary methods of establishing churches and realized that national churches could not be formed or developed in the same way as Western churches. Instead, they must be established to function and grow on their own. Allen's book, *Missionary Methods: St. Paul's or Ours?,* was published in 1912.

Several years later, Alice Luce was serving with a missionary group in Vancouver, British Columbia, where she felt called to Mexico. In 1921, she wrote a series of three articles, "Paul's Missionary Methods," for the *Pentecostal Evangel.* These articles had a significant influence on the 1921 General Council resolution a few months later that officially established the character and set the course for the Fellowship's mission.

After Noel Perkin became foreign missions secretary (now World Missions executive director) in 1927, he championed the New Testament practice of establishing what we now call *indigenous churches.* No one was more influential than Perkin in comprehensively integrating these principles into AG missiology.

## The Legacy of Melvin Hodges

Thirty-two years after Luce's writings, Melvin Hodges, missionary to El Salvador and Nicaragua, documented the primary missiology of the AG in his book, *The Indigenous Church*.

Melvin Hodges was born in 1909 in Lyden, Washington. Three years earlier his father, Charles, a Methodist minister, had experienced a miraculous healing and was baptized in the Holy Spirit. The experience led him to resign his Methodist credentials and pioneer Pentecostal churches.

Melvin experienced Spirit baptism at age ten. He attended high school but never graduated, and for a brief time he worked as an apprentice at a law firm in Denver, Colorado. At seventeen, he received a divine call to ministry. Full of zeal and determination, he played his trombone and preached on street corners in Greeley, Colorado. He was ordained in 1929.

By age twenty-four, Melvin was already an evangelist and pastor, and served as district youth director and presbyter. But even in these early years his heart was being stirred for Latin America, prompting him to spend many hours in prayer about possible missionary service. In 1935, Noel Perkin visited Melvin and strongly urged him to read Roland Allen's books.

The following year Melvin, his wife, Lois, and their three young children went as missionaries to El Salvador to assist in church planting. After ten months, they moved to Nicaragua, where they served for seven years. They returned to the United States in 1944, physically exhausted and needing recuperation. Melvin worked as editor of missionary publications, and during this time he was invited to address a special gathering of missionaries. His lectures became the basis for this book, *The Indigenous Church*, which was first printed in 1953 by Gospel Publishing House.[1]

Melvin's work detailed the ministry set in motion by the 1921 General Council and initiated by Noel Perkin. It also significantly helped set the course for missions, not only for the AG, but also for many other evangelical missions agencies. The pervasive and lasting success of indigenous church principles, however, is due to the many little-known missionaries who practiced these New Testament methods. In the 1920s through the early 1950s, AG missionaries began to aggressively plant indigenous churches around the world. The growth of those indigenous churches escalated, and in 1953, the number of AG believers outside the United States surpassed the number in America.

## Empowerment and Indigenous Principles

The approach taken by the AG in establishing churches throughout the world can be summed up in the apostle Paul's command to Timothy: "The things which you have heard from me, . . . entrust these to faithful men who will be able to teach others also" (2 Timothy 2:2, NASB).

Paul instructed Timothy and Titus to appoint elders and deacons in every new church. This practice set a pattern for an ecclesiology that acknowledges the Holy Spirit's ministry of raising up leadership. The Spirit equips believers for leadership wherever the church is established.

Recognizing a dependence on the Spirit's power is characteristically Pentecostal. Pentecostal missionaries expect national leaders in every culture to receive the same Spirit empowerment that the missionaries themselves received. What secular analysts might view as egalitarian is simply spiritual humility and obedience to God's Word. The confidence that the Spirit calls and enables national leadership drove AG missionaries to develop ministry training institutions around the world, now numbering nearly 900 Bible schools and more than 1,200 extensions in 145 countries.

## Sustainability and Multiplication

A convincing test of effective parenting is what happens to children after they leave home and are no longer dependent on their parents' leadership. A similar litmus test takes place in missions—but in reverse. What happens when the missionaries leave? At times in our Fellowship's history when missionaries were forced by governments to leave certain countries, strong indigenous churches not only survived but also thrived.

When missionaries left Cuba in 1963, the national church consisted of 290 churches and approximately 4,200 members. The church has since grown to 8,300 churches and 550,000 members.

When a change in government took place in Burma (now Myanmar) in 1966, officials forced missionaries to leave the country. Other missions agencies working there had adopted the practice of paying national pastors' salaries from abroad. But U.S. AG missionaries established the Burma AG as a strong, indigenous church.

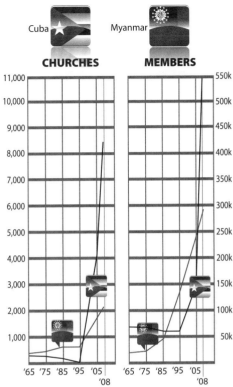

Ray Trask was the last AG missionary to leave Burma. At the airport, he met a missionary from an agency that had paid its national pastors from organizational funds. When the church could no longer utilize outside funds, this missionary had to inform pastors that they would no longer receive pay. They lost every pastor, and the mission folded. The missionary told Trask, "You people did it right."

When American AG missionaries left Burma, the national fellowship had 172 churches with 12,668 members. Now, there are 2,128 churches and more than 289,000 members and adherents.

As AG World Missions has expanded its outreach during the past five decades, a clear perspective has emerged. Wherever indigenous church principles are applied, the national church grows strong, healthy, and becomes self-multiplying. Wherever missionaries do not practice indigenous church principles, the national church remains weak and dependent. In some cases, missionaries must reestablish the work.

## Convincing Evidence

Simple but profound evidence confirms how essential indigenous practices are to the success of our mission:

- Other Pentecostal groups that share AG *doctrine,* but not the same *missiology*, have not experienced the same long-term, exponential growth worldwide.

- Dependence on the Holy Spirit's empowerment is essential to the effectiveness of a Pentecostal mission. But even non-Pentecostal groups that practice indigenous principles see greater results than Pentecostal missions that neglect or abandon indigenous practices.

- Our overseas statistics are usually quoted as an overall figure, but our growth is not the same in all countries. Some people look at the aggregate church growth overseas and compare it with that in the United States. However, success stories overseas may overshadow the failures, just as statistics of flat, declining, and closing churches in the United States can eclipse our view of the many thriving, healthy, and growing churches.

Our history reveals this fact: In countries where we have been true to the course established by the Spirit through our early leaders, we have succeeded beyond their greatest hopes. In nations where we have compromised, we have failed. We are not only our own best example, but also our own worst example.

In some countries, AG missionaries attempted to take shortcuts and adopted paternalistic approaches to planting the church, such as paying salaries to national pastors. Consequently, the health of those national churches suffered.

## Liberia and Togo—A Contrast

An example in which AG missionaries did not practice indigenous principles is the nation of Liberia. Missionaries brought nationals to a mission compound where they received food, clothing, and pay for most of the help they rendered. Missionaries paid pastors to go to Bible school and fully subsidized their church salaries. The missionaries had good motives. There are thirty-two AG missionaries buried in Liberia as testimonies to their commitment. Nevertheless, they started a nonindigenous system that was difficult to reverse.

In other countries where indigenous principles were lacking, missionaries have reestablished the church on indigenous principles. Togo is one example. National

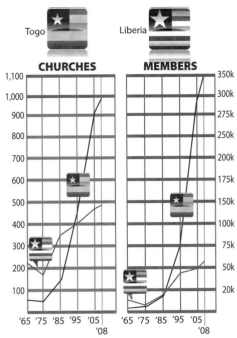

and AG missionaries from neighboring Burkina Faso started the ministry in Togo, and national pastors received their pay from U.S. funds. But in the early 1960s, Africa Field Director Everett Phillips insisted that this nonindigenous church practice cease. The national Fellowship immediately lost sixty-three of its seventy-four pastors. Transition was slow and painful, requiring about fifteen years to reestablish the work. But the national church of Togo became strong, and its growth doubles every few years. It now reports 5,982 churches and more than 350,000 members and adherents.

In the early 1960s, when Togo committed itself to reestablishing the church on indigenous principles, the field in Liberia was significantly larger with 186 churches and 14,257 adherents. In the last fifty-five years, Liberia has grown to 494 churches and 55,054 adherents. In comparison with Togo, it dramatically demonstrates the powerful exponential growth thoroughly indigenous churches experience compared to those that are dependent on outside leadership and funding. When missionaries pay the price to reestablish a church on the right foundation, indigenous principles work.

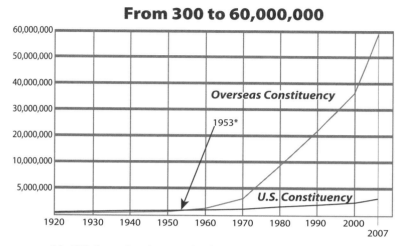

**From 300 to 60,000,000**

* In 1953, the number of overseas church members passed that in the United States.

## *From Parenting to Partnering*

As a national church grows and matures, the missionary relationship progresses from spiritual parenting to spiritual partnering. This progression became increasingly evident in the 1980s and 1990s. As missionaries and national churches committed themselves to intense evangelism in the 1990s, the strategy of partnering with indigenous churches produced the greatest growth in the history of our mission. In the last two decades, AG fraternal fellowships throughout the world have increased in membership from sixteen million to more than sixty million believers.

Indigenous principles and practices have proven effective throughout the world. The results in Latin America and Africa—where the consistent application of indigenous church principles has been the most widespread and pronounced—have been especially dramatic.

In the last fifteen years, the number of churches in Latin America has grown from 110,098 to 187,392 and membership has increased from 16,875,401 to 25,641,347. Many churches in Latin America have tens of thousands of members. About three million people—more than the entire U.S. AG constituency—attend AG churches on any given Sunday in Sao Paulo, Brazil.

The number of churches in Africa has grown from 13,953 to 45,145 and membership has increased from 2,801,536 to 13,917,391. Countries where missionaries have carefully practiced indigenous principles have shown the greatest growth.

In early 1990, the AG in Malawi had only 226 churches. That number has grown to more than 3,800. The Kenyan AG is planting an average of ten churches every week.

Churches in other regions also have experienced astounding growth. In Chennai, India, New Life Assembly, pastored by David Mohan, has more than 35,000 members and has planted more than 120 churches in the city. Yoido Full Gospel Church in Seoul, South Korea, founded by David Yonggi Cho—the largest church in the world—has more than 800,000 members.

The accelerating multiplication and lasting growth in AG fraternal fellowships throughout the world can be traced to the New Testament practices to which our early leadership committed themselves in 1921. Because Melvin Hodges was diligent to outline these practices, succeeding generations can continue to build the church on a solid foundation. While cultures and methods may change, faithful application of indigenous principles will hold true as we continue to proclaim the gospel to the unreached and establish Christ's Church.

Randy Hurst
Director of Communications
Assemblies of God World Missions

## Endnote

[1] A more in-depth account of Melvin Hodges' life and ministry was written by AG historian Gary McGee and is available on the Flower Pentecostal Heritage Center Web site: www.ifphc.org.

*Book One:*
# The Indigenous Church

# Preface to the First Edition

In presenting a new book on the subject of indigenous church principles, the author makes no claim to originality. Students of missions have analyzed with penetrating acumen our present-day missionary methods and have called for a return to the indigenous principle as found in the New Testament. Why then another volume? Simply this, that although the average missionary may have read some excellent books on the subject, yet he still feels somewhat at sea when he comes to the actual, practical application of the indigenous method.

The essence of this volume was given first in the form of lectures to a group of missionaries at a missionary seminar. Some of those present expressed their desire to have the talks published in permanent form. "We have read books on the subject of the indigenous church, but this is the first time we have heard just how to go about the actual founding of it," was the comment of one missionary. On another occasion a young man ready to leave for the mission field for the first time said to the writer, "I need someone to tell me how to go about my task. What am I to do first, and what will be my second step?" It is in response to this need that the present volume has been prepared.

It may be objected: If the church is to be indigenous, it must develop along its own lines. Therefore any set plan of procedure that the missionary may bring to his work will be of no use, and may be an actual hindrance. This would be a valid objection if the purpose were to impose a set of rules on the church or to regiment its growth. The pattern presented in this volume is suggestive rather than mandatory, and its purpose is to aid the missionary to proceed along right lines and avoid crippling errors. The reader will find that ample room is given for the development of the church along its own national lines; in fact, the whole purpose of the book is to help the missionary to assist the church in doing so.

The reader's indulgence is begged in regard to the recurrent references made to the work in Central America. There is no desire on the part of the author to impose the Central American pattern on other fields. We have drawn many of the illustrations from that field, since it is the area with which we are most familiar. There we have had the opportunity of seeing the indigenous church in all of its major essential stages of development. Then, too, each Republic has its own distinct national characteristics and idiosyncrasies. Thus we have been permitted to see the application of indigenous principles under a wider variety of conditions than would otherwise have been possible.

As to literacy, the population is approximately 80 percent illiterate in the rural districts and 50 percent literate in the cities. This percentage may vary considerably from the higher literacy rate of the cities in Costa Rica to the lower average among the Indian population in the rural sections of Guatemala.

As a textbook for the study of missionary methods by prospective missionaries, as a guide to the first-term missionary, and as a reference book for the more experienced worker, we send forth this volume with the prayer that it shall make some contribution to the ministry of our missionary colaborers engaged in the glorious task of building the Church of Jesus Christ the world around.

Melvin L. Hodges

# 1

# The Goal of Missions—
# A New Testament Church

More missionaries are working in more countries of the world today than at any previous period in the church's history. They are also engaged in more diverse activities. Along with evangelism and church planting, they are involved in the auxiliary ministries of reducing languages to written form, translating the Scriptures, and training national pastors and evangelists. A host of other outreaches include establishing hospitals, schools, agricultural projects, and industrial training.

We might presume that all the different aspects of missionary outreach are united by a common goal. Yet if we asked missionaries to define their goal, their responses would be quite varied. Some might reply that they are endeavoring to Christianize people and better their social conditions so that everyone will be happier and healthier. Others might answer that their purpose is to save souls. Still others might note their desire to witness to every creature and hasten Christ's return.

All of these are worthy objectives, but none is really adequate. Our ultimate goal and the means we employ to reach that goal are intricately related. If our goal is not clearly defined, we may err in the choice of the methods we use and fail to realize the true fruit of our labors.

Jesus announced His purpose: "I will build my church" (Matthew 16:18). The apostle Paul said that Jesus loved the church and gave himself for it (Ephesians 5:2). Throughout his epistles, Paul described his own labors as being for the sake of the church. We can have no better goal than the one set forth in the New Testament. Therefore, our objective is defined this way: We desire to establish a strong church patterned after the New Testament example. In order to have a New Testament church, we must follow New Testament methods.

Some years ago, a group sent missionaries overseas. Their primary interest was to give a Christian witness to all the earth. They based their objective and methods on Jesus' statement in Matthew 24:14: "And this gospel of the kingdom will be preached in the whole world as a testimony to all nations, and then the end will come." Desiring to hasten the Lord's return and realizing that the Great Commission must be fulfilled before that time, they decided that missionaries should not tarry in any one place for an extended time. Rather they should push on from city to city and give each place the gospel witness.

When social betterment is the principal objective of a mission, the tendency usually is to develop institutions such as schools, hospitals, and agricultural projects. These are all worthy projects. Every Christian wants to help improve the lives of those around them. However, according to the New Testament plan, social betterment is a byproduct rather than the heart of a missionary program. If we fail to see this, we build strong institutions, but the church usually remains weak.

When the emphasis is primarily social work, the church is left unprepared to meet a crisis, such as a change in government that forces the withdrawal of missions funds and personnel. Left without the crutches of foreign aid, the church cannot stand alone and the institutions succumb to the enemy. An indigenous, New Testament church is better able to survive under such conditions.

So what are the elements of the New Testament church that we want to establish? A careful study of the Book of Acts and the Epistles reveals

*Characteristics of the New Testament Church* the methods employed by the apostles, particularly Paul, the model missionary. In every city where Paul went, he preached to both Jews and Gentiles and brought new believers to a convenient meeting place. It may have been the home of a believer or a public location that was available, such as a synagogue or school. These groups of believers met together at regular intervals for worship and instruction in

Christian doctrine and conduct. Elders and deacons chosen from among the number provided the necessary leadership and ministry as they witnessed to their townspeople and the surrounding area.

Paul was in Thessalonica only a few weeks, yet he left an established church. He labored in Ephesus two years and taught in the school of Tyrannus. As a result, all the province of Asia in Asia Minor heard the Word of the Lord. His farewell discourse to the Ephesian elders is recorded in Acts 19 and 20. It serves as a classic example of a missionary's relationship to the church he has founded.

Paul stayed a limited time in one area, but he left behind a church that could govern itself, finance its own expenses, and extend the gospel throughout the region. Paul evidently made no appeals for workers from Jerusalem or Antioch to fill pastorates of churches he raised up. No record is given of financial appeals to support workers or church construction. Rather, Paul received offerings among these new missionary churches to help the saints of the mother church in Jerusalem when the region was stricken with famine. What a commentary on the effectiveness of New Testament methods! How far we have drifted from that ideal in our present procedure!

New Testament churches did not depend on workers or funds from a foreign field but were self-sufficient as local units. With that in mind, what could be said of a church today that must depend on outside help to exist? Some churches that were established more than twenty years ago and have fairly large congregations still cannot support their own pastors. One particular church, after several decades of existence, appealed to the mission board for a new pastor when the current pastor retired. A church that must follow such a procedure is far from the New Testament pattern.

In what condition would we find our work if, because of some emergency, we had to call our missionaries home and cut off all support funds? Would it be a mortal blow for overseas churches, or would they be able to survive? This is not an idle question. Over the years, mission fields have closed for a variety of reasons, causing missions funds to be withdrawn. The church must be built in such a way that the gates of hell shall not prevail against it (Matthew 16:18).

In one country, a mission faced a financial crisis and was forced to radically cut support funds for pastors. As a result, pastors left their churches and took secular employment, resulting in abandoned chapels and scattered congregations. Something was fundamentally wrong in the life of those churches. Surely God does not intend for the church in any country to be so dependent upon a sponsoring mission that it sickens and dies when help is removed.

*The Goal Is Obtainable*

The ideal of a church patterned after the New Testament model is possible because the gospel has not changed. God has not changed, and His Holy Spirit is with us as He was with the church in New Testament times. We do not propose to introduce a new pattern or system. We simply desire to return to the New Testament pattern and see a church founded that will bear the characteristics of the apostolic model. This is possible because the gospel is universal and adaptable to every climate and race, to every social and economic level.

New Testament preaching and practice will produce a New Testament church wherever the gospel is preached. People of other lands can be won to Christ and empowered by the Holy Spirit to carry on the work of the church equally as well as Americans. God himself designed the gospel, so it fills the need of the African, the Northern Asian, or the Indian. As a result, no place on earth exists where the gospel seed will not produce an indigenous church if it is properly planted. The Holy Spirit can work in one country as well as in another. To proceed on the assumption that an infant church in any land must always be cared and provided for by the sending mission is an unconscious insult to the people we endeavor to serve. This way of thinking is evidence of a lack of faith in God and in the power of His gospel.

*Rethink This Chapter*

1. What are some objectives given as the goal of missions?
2. What is the New Testament goal of missions?
3. What is the result when social betterment becomes the goal of missions?
4. What were the characteristics of the New Testament church?
5. Explain why the goal of an indigenous New Testament church is obtainable.

# 2

# The New Testament Church — A Responsible Church

The New Testament church is a vital organism with power not only to maintain itself but also to expand and extend itself throughout the country where it is planted. Yet too often churches planted by missionaries are not that kind of church. What makes the difference?

In some places missionaries have labored fifty years, and still the local congregation is unable to carry on alone. Why is it that after ten, fifteen, or twenty years of missionary effort in a given area, we must still appeal to the home churches for additional funds and workers? One missionary asked:

> Why do we still have a weak church organization that cannot stand alone, even after years of growth? Why is this church, after being organized for more than twenty years, unable to produce the type of national leadership necessary to develop, sustain and consolidate gains made during periods of revival outpourings? After studying this question for the past ten years, I have come to the conclusion that our problem lies in the failure to work for an indigenous church. Unless a church can be taught the necessity of shouldering its own burden and facing its own problems, it cannot be expected to develop, even with the aid of periodic revival outpourings.

*Weaknesses in the National Church*    George R. Upton, former missions secretary of the Pentecostal Assemblies of Canada, analyzed this problem and placed the blame directly at the door of the mission and the missionary.

> Here is a missions agency, sincerely devoted to assuming a creditable share in world evangelism. Missionary candidates and funds are available for developing the field in question. Land is purchased, and extensive buildings erected—missionary homes, churches, schools, hospitals, dormitories, medical clinics and other outreaches. Workmen are hired, and provision is made for youth who enter school. When workers are trained, they are placed on salary with funds from the home office. The missionary, whose time and energies are fully occupied with the business of managing the vast community, anticipates that this will probably be his home for years to come, so he provides for the extras that make the plan comfortable and convenient.
>
> He is the undisputed master over this establishment. Funds for workers, teachers and preachers flow thorough his hands. He hires or dismisses at will. If a church springs up, it is under his direct supervision. He feels impelled to remain as director of this, his sphere of influence and operation, as long as he remains a missionary. When itinerating, he describes the progress made, the buildings erected, the institutions operating and the number of workers employed. He presents pictures of the whole project. He may even appeal for additional missionaries.
>
> After fifteen to twenty years of this type of work, he may wonder why the church does not show some signs of standing on its own feet. The workers do not manifest any initiative. The people do not show any concern for the salvation of their neighbors or manifest

a willingness to assume financial responsibility for any phase of the work. He realizes that his removal from the oversight of the mission would bring the whole project to a standstill unless another missionary took over.

What is the reason for this? Simply the plan he followed. He treated the people like irresponsible children. He led them, thought for them and relieved them of all financial responsibility. He unintentionally robbed them of the practical processes that develop strong characters in any walk of life, wherever they may live.

Actually, he founded a sort of spiritual hospital over which he must be chief nurse as long as it remains. His life's work has become a liability instead of an asset. He sowed his leadership and domination and provision of every need, and he reaped the servitude and malnutrition of a community of underdeveloped spiritual children. Avoiding this result is difficult in a mission that runs predominantly to institutional development!

Here is the key to the problem: As missionaries, we have too often trained believers in dependency rather than responsibility. It may be because we feel overprotective toward them; it may be that unconsciously we desire to be the head and have people look to us as the indispensable one; it may stem from our lack of faith in the Holy Spirit to do His work in maturing them. For whatever reason, the fact remains that weak churches are often the product of the missionaries' wrong approach to their task. How we long to see vigorous believers who will testify fearlessly to their neighbors! How desperately needed is the spirit of dedication and sacrifice so that true leadership will develop! The "pearl of great price" in building the church is a sense of responsibility on the part of believers. With it, other things being equal, the church will prosper. Without it, although bolstered with a thousand foreign props, in the end the church will succumb to the inertia and resistance of the world. Only God can produce this sense of responsibility, but the way in which missionaries approach their task will open or close the door of possibility to this vigorous aspect of Christian living.

Here are some things that missionaries must consider:

*Is the Mission the Center?*

1. They should have a clear concept of their work as missionaries and of their proper relationship to national believers. They must understand that a missionary's ministry in any one area is transitory. It has been aptly compared to the scaffolding used in the erection of a building. What would one think of a carpenter who had to leave his scaffolding in place so the building would not fall down! Missionaries may center the work too completely on themselves, the money they bring to the work and their own abilities. They become indispensable. National believers learn to depend on them for everything. Consequently, the believers do not develop initiative, and the work never reaches the stage where it can be left without missionary supervision.

The successful missionary is one who has done his work so well that he is no longer needed in that area. "A modern missionary . . . is not intended to be a permanent factor. . . . His work is to make Christ the permanent factor, and move on to other pioneer tasks as quickly as he can. Institutions which tie the foreigner down to permanent work are intrinsically dangerous expedients."[1] The true measure of success is not what missionaries accomplish while on the field, but the work that still stands after they are gone.

*Too Many Missionaries?*

2. The development of the indigenous church may be hindered by a disproportionate number of missionaries in a particular area. To develop the abilities and ministries of believers, missionaries should never hold a position that a capable national can fill. When there are too many missionaries in proportion to the number of national workers, the tendency is to let missionaries fill all the important posts. As a result, nationals are not given proper responsibilities and fail to develop. Missionary personnel should be allocated so that they perform tasks that would be left undone if they were not there and under circumstances that require them to use national believers to meet the demands of the work.

*American Methods?*

3. Failure to produce an indigenous church may be found when missionaries fail to adapt to the psychology and methods of the people with whom they work. An understandable but

excessive fondness for the "American way" may make missionaries feel that American methods are the only right methods. The work must be administered according to the American plan, and Bible schools must be patterned after programs in the United States. Even the chapel must be built according to the American idea of architecture. Nationals find it difficult to fit into this pattern. Therefore, year after year missionaries continue to administrate according to their own ideas, and the indigenous church does not develop.

4. A frequent hindrance to the development of the indigenous church is the introduction of outside funds into the structure of the work, resulting in a *Too Much Foreign Money?* church that depends on foreign aid for its support and advancement. This weakens the spiritual and moral fiber of the church, kills the initiative of national believers, and dulls their sense of responsibility.

5. Missionaries may fail to exercise a vigorous faith in God to develop the spiritual capabilities of believers. Like a *Lack of Faith?* tropical plant in a northern climate, believers may be placed in a spiritual greenhouse. Missionaries hesitate to place responsibility upon new believers for fear of discouraging them. They may not teach believers to tithe. Sometimes missionaries fail to take advantage of new believers' enthusiasm to witness or are afraid to allow God-called men to launch out into ministry for fear they might fall into sin. A missionary once said that we could not expect the church on the mission field to take on the ministry of intercession, since the national believers were too spiritually young and inexperienced to understand it!

We must establish genuinely indigenous churches because the church of Jesus Christ in Northern Asia, *Not a Dependent Church* Latin America or Africa is not, and should not be, a branch of the American church. It must be a church in its own right. We should plant the gospel seed and cultivate it in such a way that it will produce the Asian or African church. We must train the national church in independence rather than dependence. A church that must depend on missionaries for its workers, call for additional missionaries to extend the work, or plead for outside funds in order to keep going is not an indigenous church. Instead, it is a hothouse plant that must have an artificial atmosphere and receive special care in order to stay alive. When we find ourselves in a situation like this, let us examine the type of work we are doing. Let us ascertain why we are building a work that cannot progress without artificial help. Surely the weak thing we have produced is not what Jesus meant when He said, "I will build my church; and the gates of hell shall not prevail against it" (Matthew 16:18, KJV).

Missionaries must have not only the right concept of their ministry, but also faith in the power of the gospel to do for others what it has done for them. In the early days of Pentecost in the United States, believers went out with hearts aflame to preach the gospel. God honored them with ministries and gifts of the Spirit. Can we have faith in God to do the same for others today, regardless of where they live? Or do we doubt His power to work in this way in other lands?

## Rethink This Chapter

1. Why are churches planted by missionaries sometimes unable to assume their true responsibilities?
2. How important is a sense of responsibility in the local church?
3. What are some reasons that a church becomes too dependent on a missionary?
4. Explain how a missionary's faith is important in establishing a strong national church.

## Endnote

[1] Alexander McLeish, "The Effective Missionary," in Sidney J. W. Clark, *The Indigenous Church*, p. 6.

# 3

# Self-Government

Three basic elements that make the church indigenous are self-propagation, self-support, and self-government. Should any of these essential elements be missing, the church is not truly indigenous. But how can the missionary assure the development of these necessary factors in the national church?

Of these three aspects, self-government is the most difficult and requires the longest time to achieve. Yet the principle of self-government is so important—and the result in the spiritual life of the church so vital—that failure to achieve it could well mean failure of the entire program of establish-

*Importance of Self-Government*

ing the indigenous church. Self-government creates a sense of spiritual responsibility that is reflected in self-support and self-propagation. Failure to place the responsibility of self-government on believers chokes their initiative and dwarfs their spiritual growth. Furthermore, the rising tide of nationalism worldwide demands that the national church be freed from the missionary domination. National believers doubtless welcome the missionary's leadership in the beginning, but they will not be content long if church management remains in foreign hands.

If the missionary fails to recognize this legitimate desire for independence and work along with it, dissatisfaction results. Then an ultranationalistic agitator may come along. Because believers do not have their proper place in the work, frustration buried deep in their hearts come to the surface, creating the makings of a division. The dissatisfied group may even decide to split off in order to govern its own affairs. Many such splits can be avoided by taking the proper steps to establish self-government.

George Upton wrote:

> To assume that any [national] church perpetually requires constant supervision by a missionary is an unintended insult to [believers'] capacity to manage their own affairs. The most primitive [peoples] have some form of local and tribal government, adjusted to existing conditions. Necessity and common sense, even among the most backward and primitive, have so required. How much more then may those same [nationals], now washed by the blood of Calvary's Lamb, enlightened with the Word of God and filled with the Holy Ghost, give wise administration to the church and community.[1]

Perhaps we have made the mistake of thinking of self-government primarily on a national level rather than in terms of the local church. A national organization in the hands of inexperienced believers would, in the beginning, present almost insurmountable obstacles. But government of local churches according to the New Testament pattern is not beyond their capacity, even though they may have limited training or educational advantages. Hundreds of local assemblies were organized in the Early Church before the apostles and elders came together in Jerusalem for the first "General Council."

*Self-Government Begins with the Local Church*

In some areas, it appears we have started at the wrong level.[2] We have set up an organization at the top, among missionaries and perhaps a small number of the most capable workers, and hoped that in time organized self-government would filter down to the local church. But in order to have any real foundation in self-government, we must begin with the local church. While this may be a slower process, it is nevertheless simpler, and the organizational structure will be built on a firmer foundation.

Properly functioning local churches are the fundamental units of a united fellowship. If missionaries organize believers into local churches, they have a powerful medium for evangelism and the essential basis for self-government. No matter how many new believers or workers there are, if they are not enabled to form local, self-governing churches, then an indigenous church does not exist. The first step in self-government is the founding of properly organized local churches throughout the district. Any national organization that may exist later is for the purpose of serving the local churches and aiding in the extension of the work beyond the local sphere.

The establishment of the first local church casts a mold for the pattern that subsequent churches will likely follow. Therefore, a good beginning is of utmost importance. Otherwise, changes must be made later, and changes are difficult. The foundation of self-government should *Necessity of Right Beginning* be laid with the first church. If the missionary makes all the decisions at the beginning, believers will become accustomed to his leadership. Later, when they should take the responsibility of managing their own affairs, they will be unable and even unwilling to do so.

"The temptation (to the missionary) to carry on certain features of the government of the church is almost irresistible. Is the missionary not the father of the church? . . . Therefore, the various items related to the government of the church from the very start have been indicated by the wisdom of the missionary. It is difficult for the nationals to carry on the work independent of the missionary. They have from the start depended on his wisdom, and they continue to do so as the church grows. It is only the energy of the Holy Spirit coupled with resistance within the soul of the missionary that will turn over all the factors involved in the government of the church—all its committees, its treasureship, trusteeship, its discipline, its preaching and teaching functions — to the nationals. All of it must be by the local members."[3]

Having won a group of believers, a missionary must shift his or her role from being an evangelist to an instructor on the precepts of the Christian faith and the standards of Christian living. The Great Commission emphasizes the teaching aspect of the missionary's ministry: "Go ye therefore and *teach* all nations" (Matthew 28:19, KJV; emphasis added). The objective of the teaching is to enable believers to arrive at a clear understanding of Christian faith and conduct.

**Agreement on Fundamentals**    Without a standard of doctrine and conduct accepted in common by believers, a true Christian church will not emerge. Every established congregation, including groups that do not profess to believe in a creed or organization, has some kind of written or unwritten standard. They have a common understanding and agreement regarding points they consider vital.

To say that the Bible alone is the basis of fellowship is scarcely sufficient. No region, however isolated, is so remote that it is safe from the presence of false teachers. Many religious groups say they are guided by the Bible.

Agreement on certain basic points is fundamental to fellowship (1 Corinthians 1:10). In the Assemblies of God, the common basis is our statement of fundamental truths. For example, there is common agreement that a person must be born of God's Spirit before he may become a member of a church. He must also "bring forth fruits" (Matthew 3:8) that indicate true repentance and a genuine experience with God.

When our missionary first went to El Salvador, Central America, he found independent groups of believers without church government or discipline. Everyone did what was right in his own eyes. All manner of unhealthy and unscriptural practices and beliefs were evident among the new believers.

Some of these believers desired a higher standard of Christian living. They came to the missionary, and together they studied the situation and reached certain conclusions concerning standards for church membership. One of the principal decisions was to require legal marriage instead of the common-law tradition prevalent in the country. They also decided on church practice and made a statement of basic doctrine. These agreements and the Scripture references supporting them were published in a pamphlet and became the guide for establishing local congregations, exercising church discipline, etc. From that beginning the churches made rapid strides in self-propagation, self-support, and self-government. This never could have resulted if the believers had failed to reach a basis of agreement.

It is vital that believers themselves reach an understanding of the Christian life, based on the Scriptures, so that their faith is firmly grounded and they are able "to give an answer to everyone who asks you to give the reason for the hope that you have" (1 Peter 3:15). Then they are prepared to work together as a church. The agreement need not be published in pamphlet form (though such a tool is convenient). A list of Scripture references under appropriate headings, left on record in the church, will suffice.

One point deserves special emphasis. The standard of doctrine and conduct must be an expression of the believers' own concept of the Christian life as they find it in the Scriptures. Knowing the missionary's belief is not enough. This is a vital distinction. Nothing is gained by taking our ideas and forcing them on others as if to say, "Here is our set of rules. If you are to be a member of our church, this is what you must do."

Instead, we must come together and patiently sit with them, a day or a year as the occasion requires, until we have reached an understanding. It is to be their church and their standard. They will carry on after we are gone. If the church is established according to the missionary's standard and not their own, the believers will do nothing to see that it is enforced when the missionary is not there. But if the truth of Scripture has gripped their minds, they will say, "We must do this, not because the missionary says so, but because God's Word teaches it."

Once believers agree on the standard of membership in a proposed church, the second step is choosing charter members. The missionary will request believers to make known their desire to become members of the kind of church they have studied. Then, with the consent of the group, he may choose three or four who are dependable and mature to serve with him as an examining committee.

*Charter Members*

This committee will review the list of candidates for membership. Each candidate will be examined as to his or her Christian experience, testimony, and faithfulness. This question should be asked: "[Name] desires to be a member. Should he or she be accepted?" As the names are mentioned, the missionary should try to arrive at the committee's true opinion. This requires patience and tact. People of other cultures often are not noted for their frankness. Sometimes they will readily answer, "Yes, this man is very sincere and faithful." Yet the response really stems from a reluctance to express themselves. The missionary may need to do a bit of tactful probing. He may find it wise to leave the committee alone to discuss the matter among themselves for a moment. Perhaps the decision will be that the candidate should wait a little longer and give further proof of his or her sincerity.

In all this the missionary will be counseling and guiding, but not compelling. The right attitude will show believers the importance of a good beginning—of keeping the work pure, of not being overanxious for large numbers or trying to woo the rich and influential. The missionary is laying the foundation and must proceed with care.

If the committee is in doubt, the missionary should endeavor to guide them by referring to the Bible. God's Word is an authority they will honor, and one to which they can always appeal. In this way, they will see that authority rests in the Word of God and not with the missionary.

When the list is complete, a member of the committee will be appointed to read it to the entire group of believers. To avoid offending people, candidates who were not approved for membership should be reminded that this is not a denial of membership, but rather a delay in order to give time for further instruction and Christian growth.

The group of believers should have an opportunity to express their approval of the committee's work and ask questions concerning its decisions. This open communication, done in the right way, helps believers feel that this truly is their church and their responsibility. Therefore, it is profitable for the missionary to follow this method for church membership, even though he may be perfectly sure that every candidate will be accepted. He is doing more than accepting candidates; he is training the church in self-government.

The next step will be to baptize those who were approved. Some wonder whether a missionary should baptize national believers. Obviously

*Baptizing*
*Converts*
he will have to do so at first. The apostle Paul baptized when occasion required, but he did not consider it an essential part of his missionary ministry (1 Corinthians 1:14–17).

Missionaries will be wise to follow Paul's example. As soon as national workers are recognized, they should perform this sacred rite. Recognized pastors should be allowed to baptize new believers and administer the Lord's Supper (in cooperation with the official board). Thus the church will not be deprived of the sacraments so necessary to its growth and spiritual life. Certainly missionaries should not reserve exclusive rights to perform these sacraments after recognized national workers are raised up. To do so only weakens the indigenous church and belittles the workers in the eyes of their countrymen.

Following baptism, the names of the candidates should be listed as charter members of the church. New members will be added from time to time. They will be examined by the church board, with initial guidance from the missionary. Churches in Central America hold regular weekly classes for new believers previous to baptism. Ordinarily a continual stream of candidates passes through these classes, which require two to three months to complete. In the meantime, the majority of the adults must take the necessary steps to meet the requirements of civil marriage and be introduced into the life and activities of the church. When the day comes for their public baptism, it is indeed a high point in their lives.

Central American pastors will not baptize anyone who does not meet the requirements for church membership. "Why," they ask, "should we baptize a man who has no intentions of living by biblical standards? We do not want him announcing to outsiders that we have baptized him if he is not producing the fruit of a believer." Therefore, all baptized believers are immediately received as members of the church.

To a casual observer, this method of introducing believers into the life of the church and the privileges of membership may seem unnecessarily slow. The object, however, is to help believers understand the privileges and responsibilities in becoming part of the church. They must realize that it is their church. What a difference this makes!

After the church has come into existence, the next step is to provide it with the necessary officials. The pastor may be chosen first. The missionary will doubtless find it necessary to guide the proceedings by suggestions and counsel, but the decision must rest with the congregation. If a certain worker has been God's

*Choosing Officials*

instrument in bringing the assembly into being, the choice of the brethren may fall upon him. Or it may be that a man among the believers has recognized spiritual leadership—a man whom the others naturally look to and follow. The church may desire him as its pastor. In such a case, he may be regarded as the temporary pastor to care for the church until a more mature man is available or until his ministry develops to the point where he can be recognized as the regular pastor.

The election of deacons follows next. The missionary will remind the church of the scriptural qualifications required to fill the office. The group may wish to choose a nominating committee. Under the missionary's guidance, the committee will then present the names of eligible members, and the church can make its selection from among them.

In several Central American countries, churches have a rather useful custom of electing first, second, and third deacons.[4] Then when the church is without a regular pastor, or when the pastor is temporar-

*Providing Leadership for New Groups*

ily absent, deacon number one is in charge. When deacon number one is absent, deacon number two takes over. In this way there is no question as to who bears the responsibility of leadership. Deacons are chosen with this thought in mind so that more capable men are placed in these positions. The practice generally has proven very satisfactory. Many deacons have developed their ministries to such an extent that they have become full-time workers.

Some may wonder how, in a new work, can believers fill the office of deacon? Naturally, this is not always possible. However, some sort of government is necessary, even in the newest church, so a temporary board may need to fill the gap.[5] This temporary board serves until brethren of spiritual maturity develop in the church. Then a regular board is elected.

Such temporary measures are often necessary when revival sweeps an area. Groups of believers spring up with no experienced workers available. These groups cannot drift along without leadership, and many new churches have developed splendidly under the leadership of temporary boards.

The apostle Paul committed his converts to the care and guidance of the Holy Spirit and to the grace of God. He did not think it was necessary to continue with them for long periods of time in order to keep them from failure. If we exercise faith in God, He will help both them and us.

If a congregation springs up in the same locality where a missionary resides and there is no local pastor, the missionary must exercise special care. He must not continue to make all the decisions for the congregation or do all the preaching year after year, since antagonism may result. He also risks the danger of spoiling the people to the point that they will not accept anyone except a missionary as their pastor. Compared with the preaching ministry and efficient administration of the missionary, the abilities of an inexperienced national worker will likely appear quite deficient. To prevent the development of such a situation, the missionary will do well to choose, early in the life of the new church, a deacon or brother who shows promise of usefulness. With the consent of the congregation, this believer will receive at least partial responsibility for the work. The missionary should explain his own responsibilities to other towns and villages of the district and point out that he will fail in his mission if he is required to give all of his time to the care of one church. When the matter is presented in this light, believers will more readily accept the appointed assistant.

Under this arrangement, the missionary may need to continue his guidance for a time. He will help occasionally with preaching, but he should plan to withdraw more and more from local affairs until he can leave them entirely in the hands of the congregation. Frequent, extended trips into the district will help him withdraw, and believers will become accustomed *Withdrawl of Missionary from Local Church* to the national pastor's leadership. Here is where the missionary should sincerely try "to work himself out of a job." He is building a church, and a church must have its own national pastor to be complete.

As a congregation assumes the responsibility of self-government, it is important to show the national pastor the steps in maintaining good relations with the official board and congregation as well as efficient administration of the church.

Holding regular business sessions is an important step. Sessions should be held at least once a month, first with the official board, then with the membership. The pastor should receive instructions regarding elementary parliamentary procedure and personal attitude when presiding over the sessions. This will help him avoid the pitfalls of profitless discussion and angry tempers.

The private session with the official board may be held the week before the general session with the congregation. A secretary should keep

*Business Sessions*

a record of the proceedings in both sessions, and these minutes should be filed with the church records. The pastor will preside at the session of the official board unless otherwise agreed upon. After prayer, he will read a list of the matters to be discussed and ask the board members for any points of discussion to add to the list. When the agenda is complete, he will present the first point for discussion. When a decision is reached, discussion passes to the next point. Generally the points to be discussed will include approval of candidates for baptism, cases of discipline when sins have been committed by members of the congregation, counsel and exhortation to those requesting advice or needing spiritual help, difficulties that have arisen within the congregation, and plans to benefit the local church.

Even though the pastor may not be aware of any special problems, he should call the church board for a session at the regularly appointed time. Often problems exist of which he is not aware. Should there be no problems, time spent in prayer and intercession for the spiritual progress of the church will be of great profit to the whole church and enrich the harmony among the leaders.

In the general session, the secretary will read the minutes of the previous session, give the financial report, and read the decisions made in the private session of the official board. Candidates approved for baptism and members to receive discipline are publicly announced. Approval of the board's action in these cases are given by voting. Any member should have liberty to ask questions or suggest matters for discussion by the entire church body. The church, by voting, can disapprove of the decision of the church board or request reconsideration of a question.

When present in a session—and especially if called upon to preside—the missionary should encourage correct procedure without being overly insistent on the intricacies of parliamentary law. He must be prepared for a considerable amount of informal discussion and encourage full and free examination of all doubtful points in order to arrive at a satisfactory solution. Above all, his teaching and example must emphasize that differences of opinion need not cause a rift in spiritual unity and that Christians can learn to express their opinions without indulging in carnal and personal feelings.

An essential aspect of self-government is the discipline of members, often a difficult and unpleasant task. Let the missionary beware of acting alone in questions of discipline. This responsibility should be shared by the entire church. A missionary zealous for the church's good name

*Responsibility for Discipline*

may feel that the question of discipline is too difficult for inexperienced Christians and decide to act on behalf of the church. In following this course, he may attempt to investigate the case. If he finds that the report is true, he may prematurely instruct the secretary to strike the offender's name from the membership list or restrict his or her privileges for a certain time.

What is the result of such a procedure? Discipline so administered is usually ineffective. The offender has influence; his relatives and friends are members of the church. Often they will openly sympathize with him. Officials who carry out the order escape personal responsibility by saying that they merely carried out the missionary's instructions. As a result, the church does not back up the missionary in his action, the church's reputation is not cleared nor the offender truly disciplined. He did not smart under the disapproval of his fellow Christians. Instead of the church dealing out discipline as a body, the situation degenerated into a personal difference between the offender and the missionary. Consequently, the church lags in spiritual development and becomes less competent to handle such cases. The good that the missionary hoped to achieve by taking the matter in his own hands did not take place, since the church was not purged by true repentance from the leaven of sin that contaminated it.

On the other hand, examples are easily found where churches, left to their own devices, lapsed into moral indifference and failed to exercise necessary restraint upon sinning members. What is to be done in such a case? Roland Allen, in *Missionary Methods: St. Paul's or Ours?*, presents the case well:

> Nevertheless, when individuals broke through all bounds and committed flagrant offenses he [the apostle Paul] did not hesitate to insist upon the need of discipline. There is a point at which the conscience of the whole church ought to be stirred to protest, when for the church to pass over an offense in silence is to deny her claim to be a moral society. It is in just such cases that the church is often slow to act. Comparatively small offenses are sometimes visited with stern severity. Horrible crimes shock the whole congregation, but none dares to move.

> Such an offense was committed at Corinth, . . . Paul could not avoid moving in the matter, but he obviously did so with great reluctance. It is quite clear that he was determined in the last resort to take action himself, but it is equally clear that he was most anxious to avoid it. He wished the church to realize its responsibility, and to act as a body. . . . He wrote to accuse the church of its failure to realize its duty in the matter. In a case of this kind, according to his view, the church, as a church, had a duty to perform—a duty to the offender and a duty to itself. To shirk that duty was criminal. Therefore he waited to see if the church would do its duty before he interfered himself. In the result, the church did respond to his exhortation, the offender was excommunicated by the majority, he accepted his discipline, he repented, he was restored. . . .

> We look upon the sting of excommunication as exclusion from spiritual privileges; but the man who

so acts as to incur excommunication is often the last person to feel the sting. His spiritual apprehension has already been deadened before he falls into sin. What he needs is the public censure of the majority of his fellow-churchmen to awaken his conscience. If the majority of his fellow-churchmen do not avoid him and cast him out, it is little use for a formal sentence of exclusion from church privileges to be issued against him and carried out by officials of the (mission) society alone. That does no good; it very often only does harm. It hardens the man without humbling or instructing him.

Moreover, an act of this kind is done not only for the good of the offender, but [also] for the good of the church. It is meant to clear the church's good name, which has been sullied by the act of one of its members. . . . But if the majority feel that they have not a real share in the action of the church, if they do not heartily and sincerely realize that the act is their own act, if they consequently do not support it, then there is no real clearance of the church. Nominally the man is excommunicated . . . but if in fact, this has only been the act of a few officials, then in reality there is no clearance. Christians and heathen alike recognize that the leaders of the church have expressed their disapproval. Christians and heathen alike recognize that the body has done nothing of the kind.

In this case at Corinth we see St. Paul's principle of mutual responsibility again enforced, and he enforced it by staying away from Corinth until the church had realized and executed its duty. . . . *Disciplining the Church* Paul stirred and educated the conscience of the whole Corinthian church. If he had sent a letter of excommunication to the church, none of those effects would have followed. . . . He threw upon

> them the responsibility and trusted to them to learn
> in what way it was to be fulfilled. In the last resort,
> he threatened to intervene if they refused to do their
> duty, but it was only after he had exercised all his
> powers to make intervention unnecessary.
>
> Therefore he succeeded through failure where
> we often fail through succeeding. We exercise disci-
> pline and leave the church undisciplined. He disci-
> plined the church; we discipline individuals. He left
> the church, and it stood, tottering on its feet, but still
> standing; we leave the church without any power of
> standing at all. [6]

We have seen very satisfactory results from placing the problems
and responsibility of discipline directly upon the church. Rather than
this resulting in moral laxity in the church, national believers are
inclined to be more rigid in their disciplinary action than the missionaries would have been; so much so, that when we have been called upon
for counsel, we have more often found it necessary to stress the need
for the spirit of grace in dealing with the offender, rather than to exhort
them not to pass lightly over an offense.

National believers know their own people and have a way of
arriving at the facts of a case that would be almost impossible for an
outsider. By making the church responsible for disciplining its members, the missionary avoids many a costly mistake and at the same time
increases the sense of responsibility among the members.

The official church board can serve as an investigating committee,
passing along to the church body its recommendations on the action to
be taken. Thus the church as a body acts in the case, pronouncing the
disciplinary action without the necessity of scandalous details being
made known to immature members.

Some churches follow the unwise custom of secretly taking the
name of an offending member off the church roll. This practice not
only lays the pastor or officials open to charges of personal prejudice,
but it also is completely ineffective in bringing about repentance in the

individual concerned and clearing the good name of the church. To be effective, discipline must be applied by the majority of the church body. In this way, it indeed preserves the norm of the church and often restores the offender.

## Rethink This Chapter

1. Explain the importance of self-government in the national church.
2. What is the relationship between the rising tide of nationalism and the necessity for self-government in the national church?
3. Where should self-government begin?
4. Explain the importance of organizing the local church if the work is to be indigenous.
5. When should self-government be initiated?
6. What is the first step in bringing believers together as a church?
7. How does a church go about reaching an agreement regarding standards of doctrine and conduct?
8. How are charter members of a church chosen?
9. How should a missionary endeavor to keep national believers from making an unwise decision?
10. What procedure should be established for receiving new believers as members after a church is established?
11. Why is it important to give believers a voice in forming the church?
12. Who should normally baptize new believers?
13. How are pastors and deacons chosen?
14. What may be done in a new work to establish self-government when new believers are too spiritually immature to fill the office of deacon?
15. What dangers are present if the missionary resides in the same locality as the church?
16. How can a missionary teach a national pastor to maintain good relationships with his church and official board?
17. Explain the standard procedure of a local church business session.

18. Who should be responsible for disciplining wayward members?
19. In what way should a missionary step in if the church fails to discipline an offender? How did the apostle Paul handle this problem?
20. Why is it better for the national church to exercise discipline than for the missionary to settle the matter?

## Endnotes

1 George R. Upton in *Indian Witness*. George R. Upton (1900-1988) served as Executive Director of Overseas Missions (1944-1966) for the Pentecostal Assemblies of Canada.

2 "It is unwise to organize a church out of missionaries and their families before there are [national] Christians, and a presbytery or conference out of foreign missionaries before there are [national] pastors. . . . Such a policy is apt to force the premature organization of ecclesiastical machinery on the mission field. It creates a church that will always be foreign in spirit. [Believers] come in one by one, find the foreigners in control and regard the whole institution as alien."—A. J. Brown, in *The Foreign Missionary*.

3 From a paper, "A Study of Indigenous Policies and Procedures," prepared by the Conservative Baptist Foreign Mission Society.

4 This use of the office of deacon doubtless approximates the ministry of New Testament elders rather than that of deacons, and to be completely scriptural they probably should be so designated. However, the principle involved in the practice of deacons developing a spiritual ministry beyond "serving tables" has the approbation of New Testament precedent in the cases of Stephen and Philip (Acts 6–8).

5 "We believe that we are not far from the apostolic pattern in providing leadership from among national believers early in the life of the local church. According to Ramsay, St. Paul preached in Lystra for about six months on his first missionary journey; then he ordained elders and left for about eighteen months. After that he visited the church for a second time, but spent only a few months in the province. Then for the last time, after an interval of three years, he visited them again, but again he was only a month or two in the province. From this it is clear that the churches of Galatia were really founded and established in the first visit." Roland Allen, *Missionary Methods: St. Paul's or Ours?* 2nd ed. (London: World Dominion Press, 1927), 122ff.

6 Roland Allen, *Missionary Methods: St. Paul's or Ours?* 2nd ed. (London: World Dominion Press, 1927), 122ff.

# 4

# Self-Propagation

Self-propagation is the vital element of the missionary program and the true objective of missionary endeavor. A church that does not propagate itself will soon die. New Testament churches were self-propagating.

Indigenous church principles recognize the local church as the best medium for evangelism. Establishing a local church, with all of its rightful and inherent vigor, is God's method for propagating the gospel.

New believers are seeds—gospel seeds. The field is the world, and the seeds are the children of the Kingdom (Matthew 13:38). Each new believer is seed for a potential harvest.

*Every Convert a Witness*

By nature, new believers are enthusiastic witnesses. Their vital experience with Christ makes them zealous to impart their newfound knowledge to others. Missionaries must learn to utilize that God-given zeal. The church in South Korea reportedly requires new believers to win someone to Christ before being baptized. It is vital that each believer be a soul winner.

The missionary who has the gift of putting believers to work will see the results of his labors in far greater proportion than the hard-working missionary without this ability. Yet many missionaries fail in this area. They insist on personally supervising every move and are unwilling to turn believers loose

*Putting Converts to Work*

to witness. These missionaries are always overworked from visiting outstations and conducting services. Their zeal and energy are admirable, yet they work a hardship on themselves and ultimately do injustice to the work. An old saying states that it is better to put ten men to work than to do the work of ten men. When the missionary puts the church to work, he gets more accomplished, and the church develops in the process. Activity and responsibility produce growth.

We must be careful not to discourage a new believer's enthusiasm for witnessing by being overanxious to get everything "under control." Most missionaries have known those who, in their zeal, won several others by their testimony—sometimes even before they themselves were baptized. Missionaries make a mistake if they set this zealous believer to one side and send a trained worker instead. The work done by the new believer will often wither and die because the mission-trained worker is not able to take on the additional ministry. The new believer's zeal subsides because he has learned that he is not fully capable of being an effective witness. Otherwise, why did the missionary send someone else in his place? As a result, a promising worker is discouraged. The proper step is to encourage and teach believers so they can develop. Roland Allen states: "We ought never to send a mission agent to do what men are already doing on the spot spontaneously."

In Central America, churches open what they term *campos blancos* (whitened fields), or outstations of the church. Each church averages two or three outstations, and some have

*Evangelism by Extension of the Local Church*

as many as twelve. Each church is considered responsible for evangelizing the surrounding territory, or at least halfway to the next church.

Outstations have opened in a simple manner. A church member living a considerable distance away might open his home for gospel preaching. Or a spiritually hungry person may desire meetings in his home.

Instead of making outstations part of the missionary's care, churches appoint their best-qualified men to supervise them. They

*Lay Preachers* assign a lay worker to a given preaching point and make him responsible for a period of time—perhaps six months. They give him a letter signed by church officials to help him avoid trouble with the local authorities. If he is faithful in his tasks, the church usually will permit him to continue. Most lay workers consider it an honor to be chosen for such ministry and are glad for an opportunity to work for the Lord. Often they go out two by two and may walk a long distance once or twice a week to care for their outstation. There is no thought of financial remuneration—it is their service to the Lord.

Occasionally the lay worker will have an opportunity to give the church a report on the outstation's progress. Sometimes the congregation will send a small group to accompany local workers to their respective outstations to sing and testify at the services or establish Sunday Schools. Sometimes revival breaks out in an outstation, and the main church feels the throb of life as new believers come in to fill the ranks. Thus the whole assembly shares in spreading the gospel. The pastor visits these stations as he is able, but lay workers carry on without help for weeks at a time.

As groups of believers form outstations, they receive instruction in Christian doctrine and conduct in preparation for baptism. Soon they are ready to be organized into churches. The pastor of the main church will talk to them and consult with the presbyter of the district. If it is agreed that the time is right to organize a church, the group of believers quite likely will ask the lay worker who was instrumental in raising up the outstation to serve as pastor. The believers agree to tithe and provide food for the pastor.

Perhaps the lay worker has felt the hand of God upon his life and is prepared to accept the call. Not only is a new church formed, but also a new worker. He in turn will send believers into the surrounding territory, and the process begins again, reaching an ever-widening area.

*A New Church Is Born*

When the time comes to open a short-term Bible school, young lay pastors won't need strong urging to attend. They have preached all they know, sometimes using the same message again and again. They are anxious to learn more. Problems have arisen that they are unable to solve. When a Bible school opens, they will be among the first students.

If the outstation is not too far away from the school, the lay pastor likely will continue caring for it on weekends, returning to school each Monday to continue his studies. If the distance is prohibitive, the church deacons will have to carry on for him, with the help of neighboring pastors, during the four-month term.

In one section of El Salvador, an established church is located every eight or ten miles in almost every direction. At least twenty-five self-supporting churches are located within a radius of some twenty miles. Each has its own pastor as well as three to twelve lay preachers who care for outstations. New groups of believers are constantly being formed as the work expands.[1]

One church, called Filadelfia, is located about eight miles from Santa Ana. Its membership is less than a hundred. It would be larger, but it regularly gives up a portion of its members to form the nucleus of a new church. This church has used about ten lay workers continually during the past number of years. These men carry the gospel week by week into the surrounding area. As they develop their ministries, many of them become full-time workers. A few years ago twenty-six full-time pastors and evangelists had been won to Christ and trained for ministry by that one assembly—without the presence of a missionary.

This remarkable work is the product of a staunch national believer. He had little gift as a preacher, but he had a clear vision of the work of the church and the necessity of teaching new believers. He also had a remarkable capacity for pushing believers into active service. They now know how to establish a group of believers as a local church without the aid of a missionary or national official. Some of El Salvador's outstanding pastors and officials are products of this church. The founding pastor went to be with Christ a few years ago, but the church has maintained its vigorous program. This assembly demonstrates the possibilities of self-propagation.

*The Missionary as Evangelist*
Local churches play an important role in the evangelization of a district where there is already a small beginning. But what is the process by which a missionary should bring self-propagating churches into existence in a new district?

When pioneering a new area, a missionary's first and most important ministry is planting churches. The missionary must be an evangelist to the lost and a teacher to spiritual newborns. Instead of settling down to pastor the first group of believers he raises up, he should remain mobile and keep the vision for the entire district. As a sort of circuit rider, he will visit towns and villages in the district when favorable circumstances give him the opportunity. He should always give particular attention to places where the Spirit of God seems to be moving in a special way, and yet refuse to stay in one place so long that people depend on him as their pastor.

When making monthly or bimonthly tours of the field, a missionary ought to encourage national brethren—those who give promise of usefulness for *Take Promising Converts Along* God—to accompany him. If an experienced national worker from a neighboring district is already helping him, so much the better. If not, the missionary should look for promising "Timothys" to assist him on his tours. However, he must take care not to foster a spirit of financial dependence by offering a coworker financial remuneration or by assuming an undue portion of the travel expenses. The tour should be a partnership in the work of the gospel.

This companionship on the missionary trail has a fourfold purpose. First, it enables the missionary to inspire and instruct young workers more effectively then he could do in a classroom. Second, the need of the field and the opportunities for gospel work, viewed with the missionary, are impressed upon the young worker, inspiring his evangelistic fervor and preparing him to answer God's call to meet the need. Third, new groups of believers become accustomed to the ministry of a national, rather than a missionary. When the time comes to establish themselves as a local congregation, they will ask such a worker to be their pastor. Fourth, the presence of national workers with the missionary inspires confidence in the hearers.

This association also helps the missionary interpret the attitudes, customs, and problems he finds. He is educated in national ways and avoids possible serious blunders in dealing with the people.

As groups of believers form, the missionary will assume his second role—teacher. He will give instruction in Christian doctrine and conduct, encourage believers in the task of propagating the gospel, and show them how to establish churches and outstations. He will organize groups and then leave them in the charge of their chosen leaders, with only an occasional visit to guide and inspire them.

*Evangelizing the Large Cities*

Evangelizing large cities is becoming increasingly important as people migrate from rural areas to large population centers. Searching for a better life and more opportunities for their children, they come by the thousands to the industrial centers of the country. In many nations of Latin America, one-fifth to one-third of the population lives in their capital cities.

This presents the church with both a tremendous opportunity and a heavy responsibility. Probably at no other time are people more open to the gospel than when they leave friends and relatives and move to a completely new environment. They may even feel freer to accept the gospel away from the previous social ties that may have hindered him. Whatever the reason, churches often multiply rapidly as they minister the gospel to "displaced" people.

However, cities are important for another fundamental reason. The life of a nation is principally directed from the cities and their schools, universities, government installations, etc. Failure to reach cities with the gospel results in failure to evangelize a country.

Extending the church by establishing outstations through the ministry of lay workers is valid for cities as well as rural areas. The mother-church method of establishing daughter churches can be successful with proper teamwork, teaching and inspiration.

Rural ministers often cannot come to a city to pastor churches. To establish a network of churches in a city requires the availability of workers from within the city. But a problem arises since those most qualified to lead city churches are usually hindered from attending a Bible school because of family responsibilities.

A partial answer to this is a night Bible school. This program is finding success in many large cities of Latin America by providing training opportunities for many workers who otherwise would have remained in the role of a church member. With training, a worker can minister at an outstation while he is studying. Once his courses are finished, he can give more attention to the outstation. Eventually the outstation will develop into a church and grow in strength. The pastor can leave his secular employment and devote his entire time to the work, or he can transfer to another city and assume pastoral responsibilities there.

Some evangelists, both nationals and missionaries, have very successful church planting ministries in the cities by means of salvation-healing campaigns. Some abuses have occurred in this area because certain evangelists have made exaggerated claims or seemed more interested in

*Salvation-Healing Campaigns*

large crowds than in establishing the church. While this has brought a certain amount of disrepute to the emphasis of physical healing in relation to gospel campaigns, we must remember that Jesus healed the sick as a means of ministering to people's spiritual as well as physical needs. Healing also formed a prominent part in the apostles' ministry. We overlook the healing ministry to our own hurt. If the evangelist will keep his campaigns in proper balance and remain humble, God can use the ministry of healing as a powerful means of attracting people to the gospel. Large cities throughout Latin America have been touched by the gospel in this way, and dozens of strong churches have been established.

To achieve the best results from a salvation-healing campaign, these three guidelines should be observed:

1. Planning is needed to establish a permanent church. There is little value in stirring up interest in thousands of people and winning dozens—perhaps hundreds—to Christ and then leaving them without anyone to care for them. If a campaign is held in a new area, plan for a pastor to shepherd the flock. As the meetings progress, think about a permanent location so services can continue after the evangelist leaves.

2. In any new area, the evangelist should plan for a protracted meeting. Three to six months, preaching every night, is not too long to win the lost and prepare them for life in the local church. New believers should be taught while the meeting is still in progress. If the evangelist's coworker is planning to stay on as pastor, he should be the one to give daily instructions and prepare believers for baptism.

3. A particularly successful meeting may produce a half dozen or more churches, depending on local conditions and the availability

of workers to pastor them. After a campaign of several weeks in San Salvador, El Salvador, three hundred fifty new believers were instructed and baptized in water. The number of adherents included several hundred more. These believers were divided into twelve groups in twelve sections of the city. At the end of a year, twelve churches were established, with a total attendance of fifteen hundred in Sunday School. The work has since grown to forty churches. The Assemblies of God in Guatemala City, Guatemala, experienced a similar expansion after a successful campaign that produced ten churches in one year. God still uses His mighty works to win people to salvation in His Son Jesus.

## Rethink This Chapter

1. What is the key to evangelizing a mission field?
2. How do missionaries unwittingly discourage national believers in their zeal to witness?
3. Explain the system used to develop outstations in Central America.
4. How does this system result in new churches and new workers?
5. What is the process involved in evangelizing a new district?
6. What are the benefits of allowing promising workers to accompany a missionary on his itinerary?
7. Explain the importance of urban evangelism.
8. Give some guidelines for evangelistic campaigns in large cities.

## Endnote

[1] Present strength (1983) of the Assemblies of God in El Salvador: organized churches, 780; ordained and licensed ministers, 800; outstations, 2,350; lay workers, 3,319; baptized members, 80,000; adherents, 100,000; baptized in the Holy Spirit, 40,000. All officials of the national organization are El Salvadorans. Four resident missionary couples and one schoolteacher serve there. Nationals are being prepared as teachers for the Bible school. Seven national officers and zone presbyters are supported by the pastors and churches.

# 5

# Developing Leadership

The government and extension of the church in any land eventually must be left in the hands of national leaders. These men are Christ's own gift to His church (Ephesians 4:11–13). Without such men, the task of establishing an indigenous church is hopeless. Yet many missionaries fail precisely at this point.

Our aim is to develop the national church rather than expand a mission. Missionaries develop leaders for the national church, not merely helpers for themselves. Sometimes a missionary unconsciously reflects a wrong concept by referring to a national believer as "my helper" or "my worker." The national pastor or evangelist is Christ's gift to His church, not to the missionary.

*What Do We Want?*

As a mission, our objectives should include these areas:

1. A training program aimed at developing spiritual, soul-winning churches.

2. Preparing lay workers and full-time workers to lead an expanding program of evangelism and care of new churches.

3. Preparing spiritual leaders in all spheres of ministry to help carry on a fully developed, indigenous church program.

*Are We Reaching Our Objectives?*

The good results that we have seen, the consecrated effort of missionaries and the dedication of national workers cause us to rejoice. Yet none among us is completely satisfied. Even the most optimistic missionary would admit that we are only partially reaching these objectives.

Consider these less flattering facts:

1. Many of the churches raised up are not truly soul-winning agencies of God's kingdom. Those that are reasonably active and successful usually are not functioning to the maximum of their potential, while others are almost entirely unproductive.

2. Many pastors and workers produced by our Bible schools are not real soul winners and do not manifest true spiritual leadership. With some notable exceptions, workers often lack initiative and depend too heavily on the mission for guidance and financial support.

This is not intended to be an indictment of either the missionary or the worker. Yet something is missing, and neither the missionary nor the worker knows what it is! The reason is not necessarily lack of consecration or love for God, although few of us would claim that our spiritual life could not improve in these areas!

3. Some workers seem to feel that after they attend Bible school, they are above pioneering a church or working in a rural area. Perhaps this reflects the general population movement toward large cities. However, our training programs fail if the students we train are unwilling to go to churches and areas that present a great spiritual challenge. In some ways, we are training workers away from the task instead of for the task.

Our training program may be suffering from one or more of these critical gaps.

*Where Have We Failed?*

1. The gap between intellectual development and spiritual development. Too often we train the mind but fail to lead students into a full life in the Holy Spirit.

2. The gap between knowledge and practical ministry. Students are nurtured in a somewhat artificial climate for too long. They live far removed from the rugged life and the problems they will meet in the ministry.

3. The gap between the clergy and laity. Our training program should aim to put the entire church on the march for God.

4. The gap in our concept of the role that training workers plays in the church's development. Some missions train only to fill vacancies.

A Latin American minister from another mission kindly voiced his criticism of our Bible school program by saying that we trained too many prospective workers. He said his fellowship looked ahead and saw that in the future they would need six or seven additional pastors. They trained only that number, assuring a place of ministry for each student. There was no question of support or the responsibility of each worker. "You train more workers than you have openings," he said. "Then many must fill inferior places or get along without support."

My answer is that we are training workers for invasion. We do not want merely to hold our own. We want to train far more workers than we have churches. In this way, new churches will come into existence. A man trained under the selection concept is not expected to exercise personal initiative. Someone else plans for him and finances his efforts. Following such a concept will never result in evangelizing the world in our generation.

5. The gap caused by neglecting to train the right men. Leadership training must not be limited to bright young men who at first glance appear to be the best material. This is one of the fundamental errors of modern missions. Missionaries fail to see the importance of making a place for older, mature men—the "elders" of the New Testament. Instead, he gathers a group of the brightest minds, usually boys from the mission school or children of believers, and gives them special instruction. One missionary stated his policy this way: "He [the missionary] lays hold of the best elements of the people to whom he ministers [i.e., young boys of quick intelligence], and trains them into a force he can use."

These boys stay near the missionary at mission expense over a period of years. If they prove to be apt students, they become the missionary's assistants and perform various tasks that might include taking short evangelistic trips into the surrounding area to distribute literature or hold gospel services. They may be given charge of outstations. Later they are sent to a theological seminary and then placed in charge of churches under the missionary's oversight.

But often, just when the missionary begins to hope that he is providing trained national ministers for the church, he finds that deep-seated troubles exist. In spite of all of their training, his national workers are inadequate. One or more weaknesses may be present.

For example, the worker may not be able to lead a church. Perhaps he preaches well but the local people do not really accept him as their leader. Instead, they constantly appeal to the missionary or else follow the advice of strong lay leaders in the congregation whose ideas are often opposed to the pastor's plans.

The new worker might also lack initiative. He waits for the missionary to tell him to visit a new locality. Even when he goes, he often cannot make the most of the opportunities presented. He may experience difficulty adjusting to the humble surroundings of the community or feels that adapting himself to the local customs is a step down for him.

Finally, he may continue to depend on the missionary to meet his financial needs rather than demonstrating a robust faith in God.

Such circumstances discourage the missionary. He may decide that it was a mistake to train the worker or even doubt his own ability *Causes of* to train believers for successful leadership. Before reach-*Inadequacy* ing such an unhappy conclusion, he must remember that national workers are not entirely to blame for their inadequacy. Several factors have produced these deficiencies.

Since boyhood the national worker lived under circumstances that separated him from his national environment. He was trained in Western ways rather than in the wisdom of his own people. In some cases, even his style of speech was affected. Consequently, his own people see him as an outsider. They do not easily accept him as their leader because his ways are different.

He lacks initiative because he was subject to the missionary all his life. The missionary corrected and sometimes punished him when he failed to do as expected. Now, since the missionary has power to remove him from his position and church, his only safety lies in obeying the missionary. Is it any wonder that he lacks initiative?

Granted, he looks to the missionary for his support. Hasn't the missionary always provided for him—in school, at the outstation, in the seminary, and now in his pastorate? He depended on the missionary his entire life. Can he overcome all these years of training  because he now pastors a church? This is especially true when the missionary still handles church funds and allots the salaries.

As missionaries, we must seek the New Testament approach and follow the New Testament pattern. Every deficiency in our work can be traced to a failure to follow the New Testament pattern. True indigenous church principles are New Testament church principles. The discrepancies between our methods and the *What Must We Do?* New Testament pattern might shock us. We may be completely orthodox in our theology but still be a long way from the New Testament example in our practice.

Accepting an established pattern as the right pattern is easy! We think our way is right simply because our predecessors followed it or other missions established it. Yet experience is teaching us that the modern pattern of missions is not sufficient to meet the demands of the day. We will never reach the world for Christ in our generation if we simply follow in the groove worn for us by our predecessors. The New Testament approach is flexible. It leaves room for the Holy Spirit's guidance. We cannot handle all situations in the same way. Are we of sufficient spiritual stature to determine the mind of God for the problems of our particular field, or will we insist on following through on a predetermined course?

Consider these practical suggestions:

1. Workers need to develop spiritually as well as intellectually. Jesus chose the disciples—first of all to "be with Him" and then to preach and heal the sick. Many times He called His disciples aside for spiritual instruction. He took them with Him in ministry and, as far as they were able, to Gethsemane and Calvary. In a very real sense, they went with Him through the Resurrection. Even so, He told them to wait in Jerusalem for the fullness of the Spirit before going "into all the world." Too often in modern practice we neglect this phase of training. We train in theology, homiletics, and church history, but our students seldom learn the deeper meanings of the Cross, the Resurrection, and the indwelling Spirit!

2. We must integrate our training program and synchronize its pace with the tempo of the national church. Only then will its program truly

meet the needs of the church. Institutions often tend to become an end in themselves instead of a means to an end. Sometimes missionaries view the Bible school as their particular sphere of influence and carry on quite independently of the national church. However, the national church furnishes the students and is the reason the Bible school exists. Believers should feel a sense of ownership toward the training program, knowing that the trained workers produced are their own.

3. Workers should be trained to the task, not away from it! Some institutions seem to have an objective of sealing off students from ordinary life. Directors seem to feel the need to separate students and build their character so they will be properly prepared for the work they are to do. This method may have some advantages. However, can students who are kept in an artificial climate of a theological school for three or more years make the proper adjustment to the demands of rugged pioneer work?

The New Testament approach involved on-the-job training. Jesus taught His disciples, but He also took them with Him. When He said, "Look on the fields; the harvest truly is great," He was in the midst of visible need. The harvest field was not something found on a world map. It was portrayed in the needs of the sick and sinful people who surrounded Him on every side. Jesus taught His disciples and then sent them out to preach and heal the sick. When they were confronted with failures, as in the case of the man with a lunatic son, He gave further instruction. He taught them on the job.

The apostle Paul had a training school in Ephesus where he taught for two years. He offered more than classroom instruction, since Acts 19:10 clearly states, "So that all they which dwelt in Asia heard the word of the Lord Jesus." Paul did not take this message personally to all Asia. He taught, and with on-the-job training, the workers and elders raised up under his ministry accomplished this tremendous task of evangelism.

4. We must provide for the training of the entire church rather than a select few who will devote themselves to full-time ministry. An artificial gap seems to exist between clergy and laity. The whole church functions as the body of Christ, and every individual Christian has a place

and ministry. Certainly all are not called to be preachers or teachers, but all are called to work for God. The whole church is a functioning organism. We have drifted from this truth in our churches in America, so it is difficult for us to inaugurate a New Testament pattern on the mission field! We tend to train only those who will become ministers and sadly neglect the entire body of Christ—the army of witnesses intended to bring the gospel to every creature. Can we let such immense manpower go to waste and still expect to succeed in our task?

Jesus not only sent out the Twelve but "other seventy also." What place do we have for the "seventy others also" in our present training program? The apostles stayed in Jerusalem following the death of Stephen, but the disciples were scattered abroad and went everywhere preaching the Word. We miss a tremendous opportunity for the Kingdom if we fail to develop a lay ministry.

Ordinarily training programs are set up in such a way that only younger people can attend. Those with family responsibilities have no way to get training. Also, those without the necessary education have no way to prepare themselves for heavier studies. The church is obligated to provide training for everyone whom God is calling. The degree of training may vary and should be tailored to fit the need of each class.

Remember that the worker is not required to have all available knowledge to begin ministering. The teacher must be only one step ahead of the students. The new believer can witness to the unsaved, and more mature believers can help the spiritually young. Pastors can help deacons and local workers; missionaries and Bible school instructors can help pastors. Believers can become Sunday School teachers; Sunday School teachers can become lay workers; lay workers can become pastors. If all birds refused to sing because they could not equal the nightingale, the forest would be a silent place.

When a farmer harvests a fruit crop, he not only needs a truck and a driver, but also several men with baskets to pick the fruit and bring it to the truck. Multiplying the numbers of trucks and truck drivers above the amount of pickers offers no advantage. In a similar way we concentrate on training "drivers" when we need to give more attention to getting more "pickers" into the field.

5. We must not neglect older believers. In New Testament times, the church chose the more mature believers to be its elders. Some had ministry in the Word; others helped govern the work.

Can we really improve on the model given us in the New Testament? Won't we subject the work to grave dangers and weaknesses if we sub-

*The Biblical Pattern*

stitute a system of our own—even one that is time-honored and widely followed—for the New Testament method? What can we learn about the New Testament pattern?

1. Elders are recognized as men of mature judgment by their own people and are natural leaders. This pattern eliminates any question of leadership being thrust upon the local congregation by a missionary.

2. Elders know their own people and are schooled in the wisdom of their culture. They will work in their own way rather than in the American way—a necessary factor for a truly indigenous church.

3. The growth of an elder's ministry will be natural rather than forced. People of the community think of him as one of their own number, rather than as an employee of a mission. His influence will be proportionately greater. He will grow into the ministry as a result of normal Christian development, not as "hothouse" growth fostered by a mission. His zeal to work for God is the result of his spiritual experience. He desires to make Christ known and is thankful for an opportunity to preach in outstations and surrounding villages. He receives Bible training because he is a gospel worker, not in the hope that training will make him one.

4. He is already established in business or farming and does not need the missionary's support. The day should come when the local church will assume his support and free him for full-time service. Until then he is largely free from looking to the missionary to supply his financial needs.

5. Elders introduce a mature element in the administration of church affairs. They represent national leadership and provide a stabilizing influence in church government. Their decisions are formed from a national point of view—an indispensable factor in building a strong national church. This factor is lacking when missionaries make decisions that are accepted without question by mission-trained workers.

In Nicaragua, a 58-year-old-man accepted Christ. Two years later he entered Bible school. After his studies, he served as a pastor for fifteen years.

We must not overlook men like him. If we train only young men because we can mold them and give them a complete theological education, we slow the development of the national church.

J. Herbert Kane, missionary to China, comments:

> All things being equal, a man with a college education is better than one without. Naturally we missionaries would like to see some seminary men join the work in North Anhwei; but experience has taught us that these people do not always turn out well. They invariably have difficulty in adjusting themselves to the primitive conditions existing in the interior. Having once become accustomed to a semi-Western style of living in Shanghai or Hong Kong, they are unable, many of them, to 'eat bitterness' along with the uncouth people of the country districts. Sooner or later they fall sick, or grow weary in well-doing, and drift to the larger cities, which offer more scope for their talents and better opportunity for advancement. Local men with a moderate amount of schooling have no such trouble. Having been brought up in the district, they are part of the community. They are familiar with local customs; they speak the local dialect; and they eat the local food. Moreover, their shops and homes are there. Their farms and families are there. This gives stability to the work, and stability always makes for permanency.[1]

Some people object to the idea that elders with little training can be trusted to do things in the proper way. Yet the apostle Paul trusted them. They likely will make mistakes, but missionaries also make mistakes—even after years of service. Probably the real objection is that missionaries believe this type of worker introduces an element over which they have little control. But is this a bad thing? We cannot have missionary-dominated workers and a strong national church at the same time. Paul commended the elders and the churches "to the Holy Ghost." Can we trust the same Holy Spirit to give true leadership to local churches through their own elders? May God increase our faith!

Of course, problems will present themselves in training more mature men for leadership. Young men can leave their homes for extended periods of time to receive Bible *Adapt Bible Training* training, while older men are tied down with *to the Field* family and business obligations. At least some of the difficulty arises because missionaries pattern training programs after Bible schools or seminaries in the United States, instead of adapting them to the needs of the field. Sometimes a natural love of institutions causes missionaries to make institutions an end in themselves. They strive to make Bible schools into great institutions instead of using them as tools for attaining a greater end—developing the national church. If our present methods are not helping to reach the goal of a strong indigenous church, then they should be revised or discarded.

Accessibility of the Bible school is important. Within certain limits, accessibility to the student must take precedent over convenience to the missionary. Factors such as climate and health also influence the decision of locality. In an agricultural community, seedtime and harvest must be considered to allow farm workers to attend. A training program should not deprive people of their only opportunity to make a living. In a city the training program may be limited to night classes. Training options should be versatile enough to meet the demands of changing circumstances.

Also consider the length of the course. In Central America, older men come for Bible school training if courses are about four months long. Some have recommended switching to *Advantages of Short* eight- or nine-month terms, but this would cause *School Terms* difficulty for mature students in providing for their families. Some of them pastor small churches. If they do not travel a great distance, they can return to care for their families and churches on weekends. But if the term is too long, they cannot bear the financial strain or care for their churches adequately. For that reason, short school terms are better.

Short training courses also avoid the danger of overloading students with knowledge beyond their spiritual capacity. Training should keep pace with spiritual development. Knowledge that exceeds spiritual growth results in superficial workers—men long on theory and ability but short on experience in Christian living. It is better to give workers four months of study and eight months to work out this knowledge in their lives and ministries. An eight- or nine-month course of study does not offer sufficient opportunity for students to absorb the knowledge and put theory into practice.

After finishing one four-month course, students often skip a year. When they return, they have much greater capacity to receive new instruction. Consequently, they get much more help from the course than if they attend without interruption.

A decentralized training program goes to the districts instead of depending upon students to come to a central location. The nearer a training program is to the source of workers (local churches), the more effective it will be. A short course of Bible studies, taught at an area church, may be the *Decentralized Training Program* best method for strengthening the churches of a district. These short annual courses may last from one week to one month. Deacons, lay workers, Sunday School teachers and others who desire to be involved in Christian service can gather from nearby churches for classes every day during this period. Food is provided by the churches and possibly requires a small amount paid by each student. In this way, students receive training in the locality where they work.

A short course will whet students' appetite for a more complete course of studies in a regular Bible school. If practical evangelism is carried on at the same time, the short course also serves as a stimulus for growth among all the churches in the area.

Training programs must be adapted to each field. In some areas, a night school has proved more effective than a regular residential school, particularly in large cities where many students work during the day.

Sometimes a day Bible school offers night classes for those who cannot attend otherwise. Occasionally a school might also offer studies in another city, usually at night. These studies are limited, but they provide an opportunity to raise up an army of lay workers and prospective pastors from an area not readily accessible to the central school.

The concept of theological education by extension has borne fruit in recent years. Under this plan, members of a Bible school faculty travel every week or two to determined sections of a country. The students receive assignments to be completed by the following meeting. In this way, many who cannot come to a central school receive ministerial training. This type of effort can be difficult and time-consuming for the professor and requires specially prepared lessons that students can study on their own. However, the increased number of students preparing to be lay workers and pastors makes the extra effort well worthwhile.

The Bible school's course of studies should be arranged to meet the needs of the field and its problems, customs, and religious views. Translating Bible courses from U.S. Bible schools is usually insufficient. Often these courses must be revised to be of benefit.

Missionaries who plan to teach in overseas Bible schools should get practical experience through close contact with local people in their everyday life. This allows them to acquire firsthand knowledge of problems peculiar to the area before undertaking a teaching ministry. Endeavoring to give advice on problems while still unfamiliar with the background is an almost certain way to make serious blunders. An intimate knowledge of the people is a prerequisite for training workers.

Remember that personal association with national workers is a vital factor in their training. Jesus took disciples with Him, and

*Train by Association*

a missionary should travel with his workers—on foot, horseback, truck, train, or bus as the opportunity affords. Let them eat together at the same table and share the same room at night. Questions of all categories—doctrinal, social, and personal—will be discussed. Workers will learn as much from the missionary's attitudes as from his words. Through such contacts, missionaries gain opportunities of imparting not only knowledge but also spirit and vision.

The goal of training is to develop not only pastors for local congregations, but also leaders for every ministry of the church. Evangelistic, teaching, and executive abilities must be developed. God gives the gift of government, the word of knowledge, and the word of wisdom to various people. Missionaries need not only vision to detect and select these people from among believers, but also patience in developing them to fulfill their calling.

Bible schools and churches need teachers. Missionaries must thrust the responsibility of teaching upon men who have a budding gift along that line. The church needs national executives to help solve difficult problems and provide adequate leadership for advance-

*Train for Teaching and Executive Positions*

ment. Again, missionaries must thrust the responsibility for the decision upon these men and withdraw from the scene for increasingly longer periods of time. Everyone learns by doing. The only way to develop teachers and leaders is to teach them and then put them to work, even though they are not yet fully capable of performing the task. We will never let go of the reins of government if we insist that men must be fully capable before assuming responsibility.

Developing leaders, whether pastors or officials in the national organization, requires that both missionaries and national believers understand the value of free and open discussion when making decisions and solving problems. Good men in positions of leadership have disappointed their

*Free and Open Discussion*

fellow workers because they did not consult with their associates. Their administration failed for lack of coordination and cooperation.

> In an indigenous work the brethren need not only Bible teaching, they also must learn how to deal with the administrative and other problems which are essentially bound up with the life of the church . . . for the missionary to decide these matters for them either by imposing his [decree] or by the subtler method of discussion to approve his wish, is to hinder the development of the [national] brethren. They need to

be awakened to the nature of the problem so that they may appreciate the solution and perceive how to apply it to their own varying conditions, and this awakening comes only through one and another discussing the matter from his viewpoint and circumstances. . . . The democratic method of free decision after full discussion is not infallible, but neither is the dictatorial [decree]. On the other hand, it has the very great merits of decision by the [nationals], who know their people and customs; of readier acceptance and support; of correction if mistaken; and, above all, of educating the constituency in the matters of government. Without this there cannot be a truly indigenous church.[2]

Some missionaries are reluctant to place themselves on common ground with nationals in meeting a problem. They feel that asking advice lowers their position in the eyes of the workers. This is a mistaken attitude. The missionary deprives himself of the valuable contribution that the nationals can make in correctly interpreting their own people and problems. He also misses an excellent opportunity to instruct workers by his own example of solving problems by group discussion and group decision.

Missionaries should refrain from using discussion to gain his own way through the weight of his argument or the force of his personality. Usually his plan will be accepted, but no true agreement is reached. Instead, he should wait for others to think things through and never assume that silence gives consent. Sometimes even "yes" really means "no." When a missionary takes a hesitant yes to mean that the brethren approve, the problem will likely return within a few days. Nationals who are forced to make a decision that is not really their own will get out from under the yoke at the first opportunity. When the missionary is not there, no on will enforce the decision because it was not really theirs. They merely said yes to please the missionary, but their heart was not in it.

Such discussions require patience. The missionary should refrain from doing all the talking and draw the brethren out little by little. In this way he will understand their fears and the cause of their reluctance. Even when their remarks seem needlessly long and beside the point, he should allow them to take their verbal excursions. Eventually they will make a statement or ask a question that will help get at the heart of the matter. Only then will the missionary be able to guide the brethren to a decision that will truly meet their approval.

Sometimes nationals may never be completely convinced of the missionary's opinion. But then, the missionary may not be 100 percent correct! Even if he were, the better approach is to walk with them wholeheartedly halfway and stop temporarily, rather than insisting on going the entire way against their own judgment. Later on, circumstances may show the advantage of taking further steps. But for the moment, the benefits are mutual. The missionary made strides toward his goal, and the nationals made the decision on their own.

After placing men in positions of authority or allowing the church to do so, the missionary should be careful not to snatch up the reins of authority again and bypass national leaders. Most missionaries probably have been guilty of this. As the Indian Standard says, "We complain of their lack of independence, and then outvote them whenever they show a spark of it."

We teach that the church is to be self-governing, but when some important problem comes up, we simply tell national leaders what to do instead of presenting the matter for their decision. We disregard their position, set them to one side, and do as we think best. Although we talk about nationals taking responsibility and assuming leadership, yet in reality we do not permit it. Nationals come to assume that when a decision of importance must be made, we will do as we please. As a result, they fail to follow us in our decisions, producing a corresponding lack of coordination in the work. At the same time resentments develop and schisms form between nationals and missionaries.

*Avoid Bypassing National Leaders*

Missionaries teach by precept and example. Through group discussion and decision, they prepare national believers for the time when full responsibility is left in their hands. In this way they learn that they do not decide important questions individually. Instead, major decisions are reached and policies laid down after full and open discussion with the brethren, providing a safeguard in administration for the entire church.

## Rethink This Chapter

1. Name three objectives of the training program for national leaders.
2. How are we failing to reach our objectives?
3. What are some causes for these weaknesses?
4. How can we remedy the situation?
5. How does Bible training become too narrow in its focus?
6. What place did elders hold in the New Testament church?
7. How can Bible school training be adapted to the field?
8. Explain the importance of free and open discussion with church leaders.

## Endnotes

[1] J. Herbert Kane, *Two-Fold Growth*, 156–57.

[2] John Ritchie, *Indigenous Church Principles in Theory and Practice* (New York: Fleming H. Revell, 1946).

# 6

# Self-Support

Self-support, while not necessarily the most important aspect of the indigenous church, is undoubtedly the most discussed. Self-supporting and indigenous church are not synonymous terms. A congregation may be able to support itself and still lack initiative for evangelism or the ability to govern itself.

Regrettably, the missionary's use of money often weakens rather than strengthens the church. The right use of money has its place in missions. However, if missionaries were faced with the choice of too much money or too little, it probably would be better for the church if they chose too little. When the missionary does not have money, he must depend on God and encourage national initiative. Self-supporting works are in existence today that are not due to the missionary's wisdom, but because he had limited financial resources and could not offer financial help to national workers. Later, what he thought was a hindrance to the work actually proved to be a blessing. A vigorous national church was established.

Missionaries who make appeals for money to support national workers, erect church buildings, etc., should carefully weigh the long-range consequences and make sure their assistance will strengthen the church and not weaken it. The future of the church should not be sacrificed for the sake of temporary advantage. Missionaries who plead for funds and ask for outside

*Dangers in the Use of Funds*

help to do what the national church rightfully should do for itself need to examine their position to see if they are on scriptural ground. Sometimes we fall prey to the notion that the work of the Holy Spirit depends on the amount of money available. The Word of the Lord is not bound. Instead we are the ones restricted in our vision and understanding.

E. Gideon, M. A. (Oxon) writes:

> I have kept to the last what seems to me the most serious indictment of the work of the church. Most of the churches in India are not self-supporting. This is a very serious matter. Analyzed critically, it means this: Indian Christians take their religion so lightly and superficially that they are not prepared to contribute adequately to the support of their own churches and their own ministers. I do not know of any community outside India which would permit such a state of affairs. And missions and missionaries acquiesce in this, nay, encourage it by soliciting more and more money from abroad. But it seems to me that so long as Indians are not prepared to sacrifice whatever is necessary to support their churches, this is convincing proof that the church has failed in its fundamental objective—to convince a people of the truth of Christianity, for surely it is true in this, as in all ages of all peoples in all countries, that the only real test of conviction is the desire and willingness to sacrifice.
>
> It is a shameful thing that we cannot stand comparison in this matter with our Hindu and Muslim brethren. I think we have a right to ask the missions why they have allowed things to come to such a pass, why they have so pauperized and weakened us that the indigenous church instead of being a sturdy, virile, self-reliant body, able and willing to be self-sufficient, is a feeble, weedy, top-heavy administration, the members of which are always turning to the West with imploring

eyes, and abject, outstretched hands asking for alms. In this, I maintain the church has failed in its most important work, and the measure of its material success in obtaining foreign men and foreign money is the exact measure of its spiritual failure in this country.

At a gathering of the Evangelical Foreign Missions Association, Rev. Soltau of Korea made this statement [prior to the Korean Conflict]: "I am convinced that the amount of foreign feeling can nearly always be expected in exact proportion to the amount of foreign funds used. The more foreign funds used in the work, the more anti-foreign sentiment you are likely to have."

Another missionary stated, "Practically all of the difficulties that have arisen on our field between missionaries and national workers can be traced back to money."

The missionary's use of money is the cause of much resentment from nationals. They do not understand the missionary's point of view; they think he is not as generous as he should be, or that he is partial in his treatment of Christian workers. They may feel that the missionary uses the distribution of funds as leverage to get his own way. The idea is that the man who holds the purse strings is the boss. The real mistake in all this is in teaching believers to look to the missionary as a source of income.

The church on the mission field should be self-supporting for these reasons:

1. It is the Bible plan. If this were the only reason for insisting on self-support, it would be sufficient. The Book of Acts will convince anyone that this was the apostolic method.

*Reasons for Self-Support*

The New Testament includes no hint that the Gentile churches were supported by the Jewish congregation. Instead, the apostle Paul solicited offerings from the churches he planted to help relieve distress among the famine-stricken saints in Jerusalem (Acts 24:17; Romans 15:26). This is a striking contrast to today's procedure!

We accept tithing as a scriptural basis for supporting the work in the United States. We believe that ministers who preach should live off the gospel.

*Tithing Is the Bible Method*

Circumstances may differ, but the principle is the same everywhere. Why doesn't it apply worldwide?

2. It is a logical plan. Under ordinary circumstances, even the poorest people can support a pastor according to their own standard of living if ten or more families in the congregation faithfully tithe. Some missionaries object, believing that some people are too poor to support their pastor. They forget that these same people once supported their religious leaders or witch doctors.

In one particular area, the believers were very poor and the daily wage a mere pittance, yet they supported their pastors. A missionary from another area informed me that this worked because the people were accustomed to poverty. "But our people are different," he reasoned. "They come from a higher class. We could not expect a pastor to live on what the people would give him." He contended that the believers on his field were too well off to support their pastor!

If we introduce an American standard of living, we require the equivalent of an American income to support the work. If we consider preaching the gospel a profession, then pastors must live as doctors or lawyers, making their support beyond the reach of a poor congregation. But if we follow the New Testament pattern and teach that a pastor is one with his flock and lives on the same level as the members of his congregation, then there is no reason why ten self-supporting families cannot also support a pastor with their tithes.

3. The spiritual welfare of a congregation demands that it be self-supporting. A sense of responsibility fosters spiritual blessings. Deprive believers of the privilege of giving and the responsibility of sacrificing to support the work, and weak Christians will result. They likely will be inactive in evangelism, fail to assume the responsibility of church discipline, and willing to allow the missionary to do everything. On the other hand, they cherish a work that costs them sacrifice and effort.

In one city, the mission furnished everything the congregation needed when the work began, including land, building and benches. The congregation used the property for more than twenty years. At that time no resident missionary was in the district, and the congregation began pointing out the state of the building and asking for help to make even the simplest repairs. They had used the building for twenty years, so it seemed logical that they should assume the cost of the repairs. But the believers did not see it that way. Since the property belonged to the mission, they did not feel responsible to repair other people's property.

In the same country a new work started, and after a few months the believers recognized the need to secure property where they could meet. Missionaries donated some funds, and the pastor secured a small loan. Still, it wasn't enough. One of the brethren studied the situation and said, "I think that I can give [amount] more for this need." Another said, "I will give the same amount." Seeing that they were doing their best, I made a personal offering. Property was secured, and the pastor and his small congregation went to work. They repaired the building inside and out, replacing the dirt floor with cement. After a few months the building was in much better shape than when it was purchased. The sense of responsibility and ownership made the difference.

Some congregations in Central America struggled for ten years to build a church. They began in private homes, moved into thatch-roofed huts of their own, and finally—after years of sacrifice and labor—completed frame or adobe buildings. Their small chapels mean infinitely *Congregations Should Erect Their Chapels* more to them than if they were provided with little effort on their part.

A [non-AG] missionary described one section of Colombia this way: "At least 150 preaching points are visited each month. Over one-third of these centers have built their own place of worship, leaving, of course, the majority of the services to be held in private homes. The twenty-five part-time and full-time [national] preachers, who make monthly rounds, receive no salary but support themselves (and in some cases their families) by manual labor and the small offerings their people give them. Two of our congregations are taking on the support of [national] preachers, and we trust that others will be doing the same soon.

But let us ask: How many churches or school buildings would the [national] Christians have built if the mission had started doing it for them? Answer: None. When would the [national] church grow to support their own pastors if the mission would do it for them? Answer: Never. . . .

The [national] church left to its own . . . has to suffer; it has to struggle and sometimes its efforts seem so feeble, we feel sorry and want to help. The result, however, would be the same as the effect produced by the preacher who helped what would have become a beautiful butterfly from its cocoon. He watched impatiently the great and seemingly futile effort to emerge, until his good but misunderstanding heart could stand it no longer; so with his sharp penknife he cut a few of the silken cords at the mouth of the encasement. Struggling ceased and there burst forth—a shapeless, weak, helpless, ugly mass to live but a moment. . . . A rule of life had been violated. Left to itself, after much writhing, contortion and labor, a well-formed strong and beautifully colored creature would have come forth. . . . A bamboo house with a straw roof and mud walls, built with [local] money and full of people is better than a beautiful brick and cement structure built with foreign funds that has but a half-dozen in the congregation. . . .

No money for [national] preachers and [national] churches is not a handicap nor hindrance; it is a challenge to missionary ability and a policy that, if adopted generally and more rigidly, would save many a heartache and produce a stronger, more humble church in the foreign field.[1]

4. The pastor needs to feel responsible to his congregation rather than to the mission. The mission-paid worker is responsible to the mission paying his salary. As long as he has the missionary's approval, he has nothing to fear. The pastor chosen and maintained by the congregation feels responsible to his flock. The congregation also feels a closer tie with its pastor. The pastor will see that if he is to better his condition, even financially, he must build up his church. This interdependence is healthy for both pastor and church.

5. The worker's spirit of faith and sacrifice helps develop a vigorous spiritual ministry. It is spiritually healthy for the pastor to trust God for his support. A missionary can stunt a worker's spiritual growth by depriving him of the necessity of depending upon God. A worker is not likely to develop the rugged and robust character needed for spiritual ministry

*Mission Support Weakens Workers*

if the missionary constantly defends him from the struggle by supplying his needs. The mission-supported worker learns to bring each new financial problem to the missionary—his source of income. When he marries, when a baby is born, when illness strikes—he presents his need to the missionary. This creates a withering effect on the worker's moral and spiritual character.

Workers who lack the faith and stamina required by the rigors of a life of dependence upon God will soon become ineffective. By continuing to draw their missions-funded salary—sometimes for years—they produce an element of spiritual weakness in the church.

If a worker will not continue in the ministry without outside funds, any effort to assist him financially weakens the indigenous church and hinders the spiritual growth of the worker. This fairly accurate "Gideon's test" distinguishes between those who are truly called of God and those who lack that call.

One of our missionaries said,

> Pastors receiving outside aid have in many instances grown lazy and remained aloof from the financial problems of their churches. . . . A pastor who received outside assistance was asked to take charge of two small churches, thereby receiving aid from both churches and attaining a fair degree of financial independence from foreign funds. This pastor thought the matter over for a while, rather disliked the extra work involved in caring for two churches instead of one, and wrote a letter refusing to care for more than one church. From this one instance, which could be multiplied many times, it can be observed

that the continued acceptance of foreign assistance
kills evangelistic incentive.

6. In the end, the worker is better off financially without mission support. When a worker receives even a portion of his support from a mission, almost invariably the members of his congregation fail to assume proper responsibility for his support. They assume he receives a salary, even though it may be only one-third of the amount that he needs. However, it is enough to keep the congregation from feeling personally responsible.

The funds a mission has available to support national workers are usually limited and are often spread too thin to care for any worker adequately. As a result, workers fail to receive sufficient support either from the mission or their congregations. Sometimes when national workers are cut off completely from the help of the mission, their congregations become aware that they are entirely responsible to support their pastor. Soon the pastor's income is better than when it was subsidized by the mission.

This likely leads to better feelings between the worker and the missionary. Usually mission allowances for national workers are inadequate. As workers suffer, they may unconsciously build up resentment against the missionary, feeling that he should do something to relieve their distress. But when workers cease to consider the missionary as an employer and recognize their own ministries as a God-given responsibility, their outlook toward their work and the missionary is favorably affected.

7. Self-support gives the national worker an advantage among his countrymen. In some areas, mission-paid workers may be accused of being spies and their monthly check used as evidence against them. As a result, they suffer persecution. As the spirit of nationalism grows and sentiment against "Yankee imperialism" increases, we need to safeguard our national workers and churches against the possibilities of such false accusations.

In Latin America, religious leaders sometimes tell people that missionaries are paid by Wall Street and are the forerunners of political and economic domination by the "Colossus of the North." Naturally, mission-paid workers may be considered agents of a foreign power. A missionary once told an American Embassy official that our churches are self-governing and self-supporting. "I am delighted to hear this," the official remarked. "If all missions would work on that principle, it would save our department a good many headaches."

Even when a mission-paid worker is not accused of being a political agent, he may still be considered an agent of a foreign religion, preaching a foreign doctrine because he is paid for it. His countrymen then question his sincerity.

Writing of North Africa, J. J. Cooksey declares,

> The day of big things (for Christianity) . . . will come, if ever, when Islam can see men, members of its own household, who, undirected by an alien Western organization, unpaid by foreign missionary funds, will spend themselves and their all for their faith, and be ready to seal it with their blood. . . . The employed native Christian agent makes the Muslim smile in the beard; the foreign missionary he indulgently tolerates. He will only furiously think . . . when Christ really and utterly captures some Muslim heart in sacrificial power, fills it with His Spirit, and consecrates it for the task of building an indigenous North African Christianity.[2]

To understand how receiving a salary paid from foreign funds appears to others, consider this: How would we feel about a neighbor who receives a salary from an outside source in exchange for distributing literature and making converts of another religion? Would we be deeply convinced of his sincerity? On the other hand is a man who preaches from deep conviction and at the cost of great personal sacrifices. Without remuneration from a foreign source, he has no such handicap to overcome.

8. Self-support opens the door to unlimited expansion. Depending on foreign funds for the support of pastors and churches automatically limits the church's capacity for extension. If a missionary receives one hundred dollars monthly for the work in his area, every cent of it soon will be

allocated. From then on every new worker places an additional strain on the budget. Every new church requires additional funds. The missionary appeals for extra help to enter the open doors before him, but the mission board replies that funds are not available. The underlying message is, "Do not open any more outstations or plant any more churches. Do not encourage any more believers to enter the ministry. We cannot provide funds for additional activities." Surely God does not place His messenger in such a predicament. This situation is avoided when the missionary does not depend on foreign funds to maintain the work. The indigenous church has no such limitations, because it draws from the country itself and finds the means for its own support as it expands.

If self-support of the national church is imperative, how can it be attained?

Laying the right foundation from the very beginning of the work is essential. The procedures established with the first few converts in the first church will become the pattern followed by believers and churches that spring up later.

Some object to this notion, believing that mentioning money at the beginning makes a bad impression on people. In Latin America, priests always ask for money. To prove that Protestants are different, some missionaries and national workers have gone to the other extreme. They never mention finances or take offerings, at least in the first months or even years of the work. But abuse by others does not free us from our obligation to teach correctly and establish wholesome practices.

*The "How" of Self-Support*

Teaching new believers about their financial obligations to the work of God is easier during the first few weeks after they accept Christ than after they have been members of the church for ten years. By then they will see no reason why they should give, since they have enjoyed the privilege of salvation and membership for so long without responsibility. When new believers are still young in the faith, their lives are sensitive to God's Spirit and they will respond to the challenge of carrying their proper share of the load.

Believers should know what is expected of them before they become members of the church. Central American pastors teach new believers that they should pay tithes, even before they are baptized in water. Churches receive little advantage by accepting members who have no intention of fulfilling the duties of an ordinary Christian. If we teach them responsibility, we need not be afraid that they will slip away. Better to build a little more slowly and lay a proper foundation then to build quickly and find out afterward that the work cannot progress because it lacks a proper beginning. If the right foundation is laid, the growth will be solid and the benefits of increased blessings will more than repay the teaching time spent.

*Teach Converts to Tithe*

Sometimes new believers respond to an appeal with surprising enthusiasm. They enter into the spirit of hilarious giving, donating land, labor, and materials for church buildings. Some churches have given hundreds of pounds of corn and beans to support Bible school students. Others have given the "widow's mite," sacrificing literally all they have to see the work of God prosper. The liberality of believers has been a source of amazement to visitors. God honors faith, and we need to believe that He will work in the hearts of His people along the line of self-support, just as we believe that His Spirit will stir up believers to respond to any other phase of gospel truth. In the spiritual realm, the law is, "According to your faith will it be done to you" (Matthew 9:29).

Unless he receives help from neighboring churches, a national evangelist who pioneers a church may need to find secular employment until the church is fully established. A full-time ministry is better, since it frees the worker to give more time to his spiritual task. However, a minister who works another job temporarily to support himself and his family is to be preferred to one who is dependent on foreign funds for his support. The apostle Paul gives us examples (Acts 18:30; 20:35).[3]

*Pioneer Workers Support Themselves*

Surprisingly, the standard procedure followed by most missionaries opening a work in a new town is not always the best. The accepted method is to pick out a town, rent a hall, furnish it with seats, hang a sign and start holding services. The first night's audience will likely be mostly children. After the priest (in Latin America) visits the parents and tells them to keep their children away from the services, the crowd will be much smaller.

This method produces prejudice from the beginning. The missionary is a foreigner, preaching a foreign religion. He pays all the costs to plant the church. Later, when people are won to Christ, they will see no reason for taking over financial responsibility for the work. From the beginning the missionary supplied everything. Why shouldn't he continue to do so?

To avoid these mistakes, the missionary should get acquainted with the people of the area before starting to preach in a designated place of worship. As he makes friends with the neighbors and visits in their homes, he may introduce them to songs or choruses and explain the Scriptures without any formal church service. When interest is sufficient to require a public service, the missionary can suggest that an interested person open up his or her home.

It is preferable to begin regular meetings somewhere other than the missionary's home. Someone may offer his front room, or several may go together to rent a large room that can accommodate more people. In such circumstances, they feel the responsibility of sharing expenses.

As the missionary travels over the district, visiting towns and villages, he will be constantly on the lookout for people who are open to the gospel message and endeavor to establish services in their homes. This method is fruitful for the missionary and even better for the national worker, since people come to accept their responsibility for the work and are less likely to consider the missionary or worker as a source of financial aid. Following this plan, a work can open in a town without the mission having to pay all the bills. New believers do not become accustomed to mission support, which kills initiative for future growth.

Here is a fitting illustration of this point:

> One of our missionaries . . . began a new church in the village of her residence. . . . The first problem that faced her was a meeting place. The small handful of Christians naturally looked to the missionary's residence, for it was perhaps more commodious than any of their homes. The missionary, however, said, "No." They must provide a place for themselves. This

seemed harsh and unsympathetic, but it drove the Christians to become resourceful and to consider the solution of their problems without the benefit of the missionary and the missionary's resources. They found a place and, therefore,

*Opening New Work Illustrated*

the transition from the missionary's home to another place was never necessary. Had they begun to meet in the home of the missionary, they would have been satisfied to stay there indefinitely. Today these Christians have not only rented their church building, but have begun to build their own place of worship.

The next problem was chairs for use during the service. No Christian had enough chairs in his home, so they immediately turned to the missionary. . . . Again the missionary said, "No." It did look as though the missionary was not willing to share, but it was a problem for which the church must find a solution, and it did.

The next item that came up for consideration was a light for the evening meetings. They used very small lamps or wicks burning in dishes of oil. These lights, of course, are only good for a general breaking of darkness in a room or for one individual to use in reading. Again they turned to the missionary, for she had the only adequate light. The missionary gave in and allowed them to use her light. Months passed, in fact a year passed. The missionary's remark is most enlightening: "And who provided the oil for that lamp? The missionary, of course. Did not the lamp belong to the missionary? Therefore, the missionary must provide the oil." Thus we see that when the missionary finally did give in . . . this giving in was the entrance for the Christians to use something belonging to the missionary. So until the missionary left, the Christians used not only the lamp but the oil of the missionary.

These things may seem very small. One could condemn the missionary as heartless and indifferent for refusing to share with the Christians. If we investigate further, however, we realize the wisdom of the missionary in insisting that the church depend on its own resources, and to look to itself for the solution of its own problems. Had the missionary opened her house and provided chairs, the time would come when the missionary would leave and the Christians would have been unprepared to assume these simple responsibilities. Not only would they be unprepared, they would still be weak, for whatever the missionary does (in giving financial aid) encourages the Christians to remain babes as far as assuming responsibility is concerned. They would not have the privilege of doing things which would strengthen them in their own organic life. The Christians become resourceful and strong in the solution of these matters only as they are given responsibility. The wise move, and in fact the New Testament procedure, is to have the Christians undertake these things themselves from the very beginning.[4]

## Rethink This Chapter

1. How can a self-supporting church come short of being indigenous?
2. What are the dangers of using foreign funds?
3. What is the scriptural example that addresses the modern method of supporting national pastors and building churches for local congregations?
4. Explain how a tithing church can support its pastor, even though the congregation is poor.
5. Should pastors of a national church live on the American standard?

6. How does self-support affect the spiritual life of a congregation?

7. Do financial problems hinder or help the spiritual development of a church?

8. How does self-support affect the relationship between pastor and congregation?

9. What effect does financial dependence upon a missionary have on the spiritual life of a worker?

10. How can support from a mission hinder a worker financially?

11. How can a mission-supported worker be a handicap to his countrymen?

12. How does mission support hinder a church's expansion efforts?

13. Explain the importance of teaching new believers to support the work.

14. What is the best way to support a national worker in a church planting effort?

15. What weaknesses result in following the usual method of opening a new work?

16. How can these weaknesses be avoided?

17. How can a missionary make a new work self-supporting from its beginning stages?

## Endnotes

[1] William Shillingsburn, *The Pilot.*

[2] J. J. Cooksey, *The Land of the Vanished Church: A Survey of North Africa* (London: World Dominion Press, 1926).

[3] A word of caution should be given. While it is commendable for a worker to support himself by secular employment during the pioneer stages of a work, yet it harmful for the worker to continue to do so after that the church is established. Then his sacrifice is not a blessing but a hindrance, for the congregation is permitted to shirk its rightful repsonsibility; this results in the loss of spiritual blessing and vision. The church is robbed of the fruits of a full-time ministry. Furthermore, it will be difficult for any other worker to follow in the pastorate, since the congregation probably will demand that he, too, support himself.

The ministry of the worker is adversely affected also. Robbed of time for study and prayer, he is unable to "feed the flock." He has little time for visiting his members. Tired after a day's work in the field or shop, he cannot give his best to the midweek services. The whole church suffers.

Then, too, the secular work may become a snare to a worker, tempting him to leave the ministry entirely. It has happened!

Every established church should support its own pastor. Workers should be encouraged to devote their full time to the ministry from the time that the church is set in order.

[4] From a paper, "A Study of Indigenous Policies and Procedures," published by the Conservative Baptist Foreign Missions Society.

# 7

# The National Organization

After local congregations are established, plans should be made to bind them together so that local churches become the Church. The New Testament gives us the pattern. The apostle Paul referred to the churches of a province as a unit, such as the churches of Macedonia, Achaia, or Judea (2 Corinthians 8:1; 9:2; 1 Thessalonians 2:14). Individual Christians in the local church were united by the same bonds that joined local churches as the Church.

*Churches Need to Be Bound Together*

Individual believers need to understand the importance of fellowship and the ministry of other Christians. In a similar way, the local church needs to recognize that it forms a part of the Church, especially within its district or province. The necessity for such union arises from these factors:

1. The need for Christian fellowship. When small groups of believers are cut off from all contact with other churches, they tend to become discouraged and inactive. Christian fellowship revives believers' courage, brings joy in the Holy Ghost, and stimulates Christian activity.

2. Christian unity and fellowship give local congregations a stabilizing and corrective influence. An individual Christian left to his own devices may take up strange notions and interpretations of Scripture or embrace fanciful or fanatical ideas. Congregations are open to the same danger. Unity and fellowship tend to correct wrong tendencies.

Contact with other churches preserves spiritual balance in the local congregation.

3. Organization allows specific projects to be carried out that would be impossible for the local church alone. These projects include evangelizing unreached areas; establishing training centers for Christian workers; and electing and supporting qualified overseers, evangelists, and teachers who will carry out projects necessary to maintain and advance the work.

Establishing local churches and national ministers is essential before any national organization is formed. An organization that begins with missionaries is essentially foreign in character.[1] Americans must not permit their natural love for organization to make the organization an end in itself. Establishing and strengthening the indigenous church must be the primary goal, with organization kept in a subservient role.

When three to five churches are established in a province, it is time to bring representatives of each local church together for fellowship and discussion. In Central America, these meetings are called "conferences." In El Salvador, eleven churches were represented at its first conference. In other countries, not more than four churches participated in the first conference. The organization of these conferences generally were patterned after a U.S. Assemblies of God district council. Each conference was sovereign, although the national organizations recognized the spiritual ties that bound them to brethren of like precious faith in other lands.

Geographical features, political boundaries, language differences, and modes of transportation will determine the size of each district. Little is gained by trying to bind churches together into a single unit when they are far removed from each other, since no actual fellowship can be maintained. When distance, language, or political barriers make it impractical to unite churches into one district, consider dividing the district into smaller units, with a sectional council in each area.

In much the same way that charter members of a local church reach agreement on the standards for their local church, churches should come together to discuss the basis for developing the national church in their area. Local churches are represented by their pastors and duly elected delegates. Other believers from the congregations may attend as observers. These councils become the annual business meetings for directing the work of the district.

As the work extends, the district can be divided into sections. Each section may have from five to ten local churches that gather in a fellowship meeting every three to six months as circumstances permit. An overseer, or presbyter, chosen at the annual council of all the churches, oversees each section and helps the pastors and churches with problems that arise. Since the presbyter also pastors a church in the section, he will not need support from other sources. For this reason, the number of churches under his supervision should be limited. Otherwise, he will either neglect his church to care for the section, or he will be unable to oversee the section properly.

*Sectional Presbyters*

General officials—such as superintendent, secretary, and treasurer—are elected by the general assembly at the annual meeting. Nationals likely will desire a missionary to fill the office of superintendent until local believers are trained in church management. However, as national leaders develop, they should fill all official positions. Soon afterward, they will be able to take over the entire responsibility of administration. It is best that they do so while experienced missionaries are on the field to guide them, rather than after the missionaries leave and leadership is forced upon them.

Providing leadership for the national church is just as much a part of missionary work as winning the lost. The missionary must be willing to step aside and work unobtrusively as the administration passes into the hands of others.

The missionary's willingness to cooperate with national leaders is a test of both his humility and the quality of his passion for missions. One national minister said, "Many missionaries are willing to serve under the district council (composed of missionaries) but not under local committees (with nationals). . . . Unless our missionary friends can extricate themselves from this superiority complex, they will not have much fruitful ministry in our land."

Some missions have two organizations for each field—one composed of only missionaries and the other composed of only

*A Separate Organzation for Missionaries?*

nationals. This may be satisfactory if the missionary organization limits its scope to matters that affect only missionaries. But if the missionary organization acts as a supreme court and places limitations on the national organization—reserving the right of approving or disapproving all resolutions passed by nationals or exercising veto power on questions that affect churches and the national ministry—the system will likely lead to a serious breakdown.

Greater unity takes place when only one body represents the field and has the power to make decisions that affect the national work.[2] That body should be composed of representatives from local churches, national ministers, and missionaries. Missionaries may lend their strength and counsel to the work in the early stages and even fill executive positions until national leaders are prepared to take over the responsibility. However, they must recognize the proper time to step aside and permit nationals to fill these posts.

This point may raise some objections. But if missionaries are allowed a voice in the national organization, they will completely control it. As a result, there will be no national organization. In such instances, one of these circumstances may be to blame and should be corrected:

First, the work was organized on a national scale too quickly, and missionaries outnumber nationals. Second, too many missionaries are in that particular area, and a redistribution of missionary personnel is needed. Third, something is woefully wanting in the method used to develop national workers, and the missionaries need to re-examine their system.

Since churches need a national organization, some thought must be given to providing financial support for its officers. The method of support depends largely upon whether the offices are full-time posts. If not, the superintendent and other officials should retain their pastorates and travel over the field to visit churches only in special times of need. Ordinary problems can be handled by the presbyter of each section. This plan has much in its favor, since it does not place a financial load upon the churches and tends to avoid the danger of a top-heavy, over-centralized national organization.

On the other hand, the official that pastors a church and take cares of district duties carries a tremendous load. For this reason, the office of superintendent, at least, is usually a full-time post.

In Central America, pastors support their officials by sending tithes of their own incomes to the central office. Some conferences augment this through special offerings taken by each church or by tithing other church income beyond what is given to support the pastor. These points should be agreed upon by the conference.

## Rethink This Chapter

1. What are the advantages of organizing churches of a district into a council or conference?
2. What are the beginning steps of establishing a council?
3. What factors determine the size of area represented by a council?
4. Explain the functions of a sectional presbyter.
5. Who should fill the offices in the national organization?
6. Discuss the advisability of having a missionary organization separate from the national organization.
7. What are the probable pitfalls that occur when missionaries dominate the development of the national organization?
8. How are officials of the national organization supported?

## Endnotes

[1] See page 36.

[2] This statement is not intended to discourage forming an organization of missionaries in order to deal with their own special problems. Such an organization is often a necessity. However, it should limit its decisions to the sphere of missionary activity and not undertake to dictate to the national organization.

# 8

# Converting to Indigenous Church Methods

A missionary once said, "Starting an indigenous work in a pioneer field is not the major difficulty. What we want to know is how to apply indigenous church methods on a field where the work has existed for years under the old mission-directed system."

Changing a work from a nonindigenous mission to an indigenous church is probably one of the most difficult tasks a missionary can undertake. Making hard-and-fast rules adequate for every field is impossible, since conditions differ widely. In some places, present-day missionaries have fallen heir to a work founded by their predecessors. This work includes a staff of considerable size and a subsidy of mission funds for its support. In addition to considering the general suggestions given here, missionaries should read books on the subject and study indigenous procedure with a sincere desire to find the proper solution. The Holy Spirit will guide both individual missionaries and the administrative staff in taking adequate steps.

Missionaries should not grow impatient with nationals who seem slow in changing to the indigenous plan. Existing conditions are largely due to wrong training and practice. Instead, we must patiently correct our own errors and endeavor to return to the New Testament pattern.

*General Principles*

J. Herbert Kane points out that the vast majority of overseas churches got off to a wrong start, and changing after thirty or forty years of unscriptural practice will not be easy.

Our plans therefore must be carefully conceived, and wisely executed. In this connection, there are three important principles which we must ever bear in mind.

In the first place, they (the nationals) must be allowed to frame their own policies. Most missionaries today are in favor of the indigenous church in principle; but when it comes to working out the details, they are guilty of backseat driving. They relinquish the wheel but insist on directing the way. This is a serious mistake. . . .

Secondly, we must permit them to develop along their own lines. The churches of the East should be allowed to develop their own peculiar type of Christianity. It is not necessary for them to adopt our style of architecture, our order of service, our methods of work, or even our form of government. . . . We must remember that while it is right to make a Christian out of a Muslim, it is wrong to make an American out of a Chinese.

And last, but not least, they should be allowed to proceed at their own pace. Many a fine missionary has broken his health and his heart trying to speed up the people of the East. It cannot be done; so the missionary, if he is wise, will come to this conclusion early in his ministry, and thereafter act accordingly. . . . "First the blade, then the ear, after that the full corn in the ear." Our difficulty comes when we want all three in the first ten days. We must be as patient in the building of the church as Jesus was in the training of the Twelve. . . . We, too, must be patient—infinitely patient—with the church leaders when they fail to adopt some pet scheme of ours, or when they hesitate to exercise discipline, or when they omit to send in the annual report. We must not be surprised if they are late for Sunday service, or forget about the deacons' meeting, or arrive three days late for Bible school. These are the traits which will require many years . . . for them to overcome.[1]

As a first step toward adopting indigenous principles, all the missionaries in the area should gather for discussion, with the aim of outlining a practical plan of procedure. All missionaries concerned should be present, since harmony of spirit and purpose is important in taking these steps. Even when all agree on the ultimate goal, sharp differences of opinion may exist regarding the methods employed in reaching it. Such differences of opinion may constitute a serious obstacle in realizing the indigenous plan. Time spent in prayer and honest discussion is well worthwhile. Patience must be manifested by all, since a person with years of experience in missionary work may not change his or her viewpoint easily. Allow plenty of time for a change of thinking to take place. All the problems will not be solved in one session or even a series of sessions. Though progress seems slow, missionaries may take heart by reminding themselves that the project is not simply a pet scheme; it is backed by the Word of God, by the sponsoring mission board and by the Spirit of God who guides them. The Holy Spirit will honor New Testament procedure, direct the steps taken, and enable missionaries to iron out their differences.

Temporary concessions may be necessary to avoid disrupting the established work. The unknown and different factors on each field make it unwise to lay down inflexible rules. Each missionary is a member of Christ's body, and the Holy Spirit will surely guide into all truth when everyone has a sincere desire to do His will. All missionaries likely will agree to the proposal that all new works must be established on indigenous principles. Missionaries who desire to extend these principles to an established work can trust that the blessings from the new works will overflow into established ones. Perhaps those in charge will see that they are missing great blessings and be amenable to change.

Assuming that the missionaries are in favor of following indigenous principles, the second step is to prepare the nationals for the changes to

*Inspire National Workers*

come. This takes place by showing them the advantages and importance of indigenous methods. Again, patient teaching and discussion is needed. As missionaries, we are largely responsible for their viewpoint by training them to depend on us. We must now retrain them in independence and initiative.

Some missionaries decide that the work should become indigenous, announce that the work is self-supporting from that time forward, and suddenly cut off all worker support. But the problem is greater than a worker's financial support. Initiative for evangelism and leadership must spring from within the national's own spirit and needs time to develop.

In a family, a parent instructs, counsels, and guides his son, all the while increasing the child's responsibilities and allowing more liberty in making decisions. Eventually the time comes when the son is capable of making his own way. In the church family, we make the mistake of training national workers in dependence. Therefore, we must take steps to adopt indigenous principles, but we also must give national believers time to find their own feet. Otherwise, they will suddenly feel orphaned.

The more fainthearted and less aggressive workers may view the idea of national leadership and responsibility with considerable alarm. Having always depended on a salary from the mission, they will need courage and faith to step out without that support. Some workers are so fearful of being left without the mission's financial backing that they fail to adopt the missionary's suggestions. They do not encourage the local congregation to do its best in giving, fearing that their salary will be cut off as a result.

To encourage self-support, a certain missionary offered to match the amount local congregations gave their pastor, up to the maximum of four pounds. Above this amount, foreign funds would be reduced in proportion to increased local offerings.

"Imagine our surprise when in only a month or two practically every pastor had increased local offerings as much as two or three pounds so that he might receive the maximum foreign matching," the missionary said. "Imagine our further surprise as time passed when we observed that these local pastors held their church giving at this peak without endeavoring to carry it further still to financial independence."

It will be next to impossible for a missionary to develop a self-supporting church if the worker in charge is not sympathetic to the idea. Nationals must catch the vision themselves.

However, convincing nationals of the benefits of the indigenous method is easier than some missionaries suppose. Missionaries may be surprised at how eagerly nationals grasp the possibilities. As they are inspired with the vision of evangelism through national initiative and see the opportunities for leadership that a truly indigenous work offers, they will thrill to the joy of spiritual self-fulfillment. Most workers will make greater sacrifices and dedicate themselves more fully to the work of God when inspired by the opportunity of filling a vital place in the church of God than they will for the sake of a mere salary.

The third step is to accompany teaching with appropriate action. The long-range indigenous program calls for the development of all the ministries a church needs—pastors, teachers, evangelists, and executives. All must be supplied from among the believers themselves, *Planning for Financial Independence* and all phases of the national church must become completely self-supporting. Transitioning from a mission-supported and directed work to a completely indigenous church may require adopting certain temporary measures. Complete change may not happen with one stroke.

In adopting temporary measures, don't grow discouraged with the main plan or lose sight of the goal. Continue to pray, teach, and believe. At the same time beware, lest temporary measures become permanent policies. Our objective must be unalterable. The methods, however, may be fluid, requiring revision from time to time to meet the exigencies of changing conditions. It may sometimes be necessary to stop short of our final goal, temporarily, to enable the national brethren to come along with us in our thinking. Since indigenous church principles require that national leaders think for themselves, the steps taken should have their general approval.[2]

An initial action that might readily obtain everyone's approval is a "hold-the-line" policy regarding use of foreign funds to support national

*Teach Local Congregations*
workers. At that point, the church will seek to use national sources to meet needs that arise without employing additional outside funds. Steps should be taken to develop local sources to support workers who are dependent on mission funds. Each organized church must be responsible to support its pastor, meaning that local congregations must learn indigenous principles.

If they have not already done so, churches should be properly organized with their own board and pastor. After teaching and explaining, missionaries may want to hold business sessions with the board and the entire church, urging them to come to a conclusion concerning pastoral support. In some cases, believers may need time for study and decision. The date set for them to assume complete responsibility may be postponed for three to six months. Another approach is to reduce the worker's present salary by one-third every three months until he is completely dependent upon the local church. The procedure is sometimes compared to cutting off a dog's tail an inch at a time so it won't hurt so much! Nevertheless, the plan has worked successfully in numerous instances.

The preferred use of foreign funds is to offer temporary aid by renting or constructing a building for a struggling local church, rather than helping to pay the pastor's salary. When assistance in salary is needed for a time, it is better to pay the money into the local church treasury. The pastor then receives help from the church treasury rather than directly from the mission. This avoids the idea that the worker is supported by the mission, and a healthier relationship develops between pastor and congregation.

Occasions sometimes arise when a brother is in critical need. In such cases, the duty of the missionary—as well as the entire church

*Helping a Needy Worker*
constituency—is to help. Why should the missionary alone assume the responsibility of showing Christian charity? Shouldn't the members of the church and neighboring congregations also respond to the need of a brother in distress? If the matter is brought to their attention, believers will gladly

help a brother. The missionary, as a brother in Christ, may also share in this gift. In such cases of pressing need, offering a gift to help a worker through a crisis is better than promising him a monthly allowance. He can thank God for supplying his need through your gift and continue on his way in faith, anticipating that God will care for him.

In the fourth step, national leaders should have a say regarding how money should be used to develop and maintain a work. This is particularly true of money that comes from local sources. Missionaries should not decide questions such as which evangelist should be chosen for a certain task and how much help he is to receive while carrying out his commission. The executive board makes these decisions. This board should include a sufficient number of nationals to represent the voice of the national church. Criticisms are less severe when national believers share this responsibility with the missionary. Giving national brethren a voice in the distribution of funds is an important step in the right direction.

The final step in changing from a mission-supported work to a self-supporting work comes when the national church assumes the entire responsibility for maintaining the work. The mission may continue to help evangelize new territory, train workers, and publish literature, but eventually even these responsibilities will be borne by the nationals.

*Conversion Completed*

Early in our missionary ministry, my wife, Lois, and I experienced the struggle of changing a mission-supported work to indigenous church methods. We were inexperienced in missionary work, but certain factors helped us. We had a firm conviction that the indigenous principles pointed the way to victory. And since we were the only Assemblies of God missionaries in the country, we didn't battle with divided opinions among the missionary staff.

*Process of Conversion Illustrated*

The work on the field was small, but not new. Upon arrival, we found four small churches and four national workers. Two workers received support directly from U.S. Assemblies of God headquarters, since no missionary had lived there for a number of years. The other two workers were new and looked forward to receiving financial help as soon as a missionary was stationed on the field again. In the meantime, the workers who received support generously gave the others tithes and offerings from their allowances.

From the beginning, we emphasized the necessity of making the work self-supporting. We organized groups and encouraged them to become self-governing. We also endeavored to inspire believers to step out in faith as they felt a call to the work of God. They responded to our plea, but they did not make the work self-supporting. They thought it was an idealistic dream and that, given time, we would dole out mission funds to support the workers as in the past. All other missions in that country were doing the same thing.

The number of volunteers grew to about 10 full-time or part-time workers. Two of them were supported with U.S. funds. The others were dependent on what their congregations could supply or worked part time. The inequality was obvious, but I was determined not to designate mission funds for worker support. I realized that the indigenous principles presented the only road to spiritual prosperity for the work. In the meantime, the workers waited more or less patiently for me to wake up and give them the help they needed.

One day, a mission-supported worker told me of another worker's need and dropped a broad hint that it was time to help him financially. "I just told him to be patient," he said, "Brother Hodges is waiting to see your faithfulness. When he is sure that you will be a good worker, he will ask the mission to support you." He nursed the hope that better days would come.

Just over a year later, a crisis occurred. During a business session at the second anniversary of the national conference, a new worker stood

*The Crisis* and said, "Brother, my family is suffering. I have several children. I cannot continue in the work unless I can have the promise of regular monthly support." With that he came forward and handed me his license to preach. Others followed him, one by one, though in a less dramatic manner. All but four workers said they could not continue. One of these four, a mission-supported worker, tried to exhort the discontented to faithfulness. The others remained silent.

I lifted my heart to God for guidance in this decisive moment. Finally I said, "Brethren, I feel your need and your suffering deeply.

I will do all that I can to help you, but I cannot promise a single worker a salary. The support of the work must come from the country itself. If the mission has called you to preach, you can place your resignation with the mission. But if you are called of God, it does no good to turn in your resignation to me. You must answer to God. It is not a question between you and me, but between you and God. Are you called of God or not?" Then I waited and silently prayed.

The brethren were quiet for several moments. Finally a leader who received no outside help asked to say a word. "Brethren, I feel that we have been hasty. I've gone through a lot, just as you have. We talk about trusting God, but I wonder if I have ever really trusted God for my support. For my part, I withdraw my resignation and state here that I am going to put God to the test for one year."

Slowly, as God moved on their hearts, the others stood up, one by one, to say that they would put God to the test for another year. We didn't keep every worker, but almost all of them remained with us. We entered the new year with renewed strength.

But the battle was still far from won. The financial inequality among workers was a critical issue, so I wrote a letter seeking counsel from the U.S. Assemblies of God missions secretary. His response was, "I believe that we should take away the offerings from the brethren who now receive designated support. This will become effective in six months, giving them time to make the necessary adjustments. Then we will place this same amount at your disposal to help the brethren as you see the need."

*All Workers on Same Footing*

The two brethren concerned were advised that they would receive offerings from the mission for only six more months. At that point, all workers would be on the same footing. One of the paid workers was originally from another Latin American country. When he found out that he would no longer receive support, he decided to return home. I did not dissuade him—not because I did not appreciate his labors, but because I realized that we must build of national material. Unless he was willing to take his place with the rest of the pastors, his presence would not benefit the work. He returned to his own country and has done a good work for God there. The other worker took a mature attitude and made plans to establish a small business on the side to tide him over the crisis.

At the end of six months, the money was sent to me, as agreed, rather than to the two workers. I taught the national leaders of the conference about responsibility of distributing these funds. During this time of transition, I traveled constantly, visiting churches and encouraging believers to support their own workers through tithing, the scriptural basis for giving to God's work. After some months, the previously paid worker said, "Brethren, you know I felt that Brother Hodges was quite severe with me when he arranged to have my offering taken away after I had served the mission for so many years. But I saw that if I were to prosper, I needed to get busy and build up my church. So I have been working with my people, and now I am proud to say that I am not dependent upon the mission, and I have developed my own church."

During the next few years God visited that field with revival, and the number of workers increased to more than twenty. These workers met at a conference and adopted a motion that all funds

*Nationals Vote Self-Support*

coming to the field from outside the country were to be used only for Bible school or evangelistic efforts. No funds were to be used to support pastors of established churches. Little by little, the idea of self-support took hold of them, and they accepted it as basic and practical.

In that same conference, a leader said, "When Brother Hodges started to preach to us about a self-supporting church, we thought he was dreaming. We said it could never be done. But he just kept hammering away, month after month, and now look at us. We have put this motion though. It has come from the workers, not the missionaries, and we are glad for it."

## Rethink This Chapter

1. What three important general principles must be considered when changing to indigenous principles?
2. What is the first step in introducing indigenous principles in a work established on nonindigenous methods?
3. What is the second step?
4. Why might certain national workers be reluctant to introduce indigenous church methods?
5. Is it reasonable to expect nationals to be enthusiastic about indigenous church principles? Explain your answer.
6. What care must be taken when adopting temporary measures during the process of change?
7. Discuss two such temporary measures.
8. How can missionaries best help the local church during its struggle to attain self-support?
9. What is the best way to help a worker who is in difficult economic circumstances?
10. Should nationals have a voice in spending local funds? Mission funds?
11. What points are significant in the illustration at the end of the chapter?

## Endnotes

[1] J. Herbert Kane, *Two-Fold Growth.*

[2] It might be noted here that since mission funds come from missions sources, it is not within the jurisdiction of the nationals to determine the amount of foreign funds which may be used in the work. The missionaries, since they are the ones who are held responsible, will determine this. Once funds are made available for the work, the nationals may be consulted as how they may best be used. However, this particular condition, which results from the process of conversion, is abnormal. The necessity of allocating foreign funds for the maintenance of pastors or churches will disappear as the work attains the goal of self-support.

# 9

# Hindrances to Adopting Indigenous Principles

Many well-established missions are making a decided effort to introduce indigenous church principles into their work. Events during World War II convinced many missionaries that the indigenous way is the only way to have lasting results. Even so, many missionaries profess to believe in these principles and pay lip service to them, but they stop short of taking the necessary steps toward turning the reins of government over to national believers. Why the hesitancy? The answer may stem from these possible reasons:

1. The missionary may be reluctant to surrender the prestige and power that his position affords. He is accustomed to having the decisive voice and may find it difficult to turn over that authority to others and surrender his title or position. He may hesitate to relinquish control of *Reluctance to Surrender Authority* the purse strings. He knows that in his hands money produces activity and gives authority to his voice in church matters. Without realizing, he has developed more faith in the results produced by money than in the results produced by the Holy Spirit in the hearts of believers.

> So long as policies (of self-support) are dictated by consideration of convenience, there will be frequent cases in which the immediate advantages of subsidy will induce the missionary to depart from the harder

way. . . . The desirability of retaining influence over the congregation by the power of the purse, of keeping hold of a promising worker, of maintaining the status of the group, above all the desire to bind the church to his person and mission, will seem to commend the wisdom of subsidy to the missionary whose criterion is pragmatic.[1]

2. The missionary loses a certain popular financial appeal when he presents the indigenous church to the home constituency. Establishing

*Loss of Popular Appeal*

the indigenous church is the primary objective of missionary activity and should have the highest appeal to well-informed Christians at home. Yet many Christians respond more readily to appeals for secondary projects. The plea to support orphaned children or help famine sufferers will bring a ready response. The visible often has more appeal than the invisible, tempting many missionaries to carry on a type of work that makes a better showing at home and brings in more financial help.

3. The missionary's sincere desire to show Christian charity by helping the underprivileged and relieving suffering may cause him

*Honest Christian Charity*

to cling to procedures that weaken the indigenous church. The apostle John wrote, "If anyone has material possessions and sees his brother in need but has no pity on him, how can the love of God be in him?" (1 John 3:17). Shouldn't missionaries, backed by U.S. resources, do everything in their power to relieve want among the less fortunate around them? Aren't we to feed the hungry and clothe the naked for Christ's sake?

A factor that makes the problem difficult to analyze is the difference in standards of living.

"It is a recognized fact that there is a great contrast between the standard of living in the United States and most countries where foreign missionaries now work. . . . There is, therefore, the unconscious temptation on the part of the missionary to feel that he should try to raise the standard of living of the people to whom he ministers. The standard of living which he considers the norm is, of course, that of the United States of America. This is a false premise. Salvation is not a matter of civilization. It is true that backward civilizations have been greatly improved by the influence of the Lord Jesus Christ . . . but this is a byproduct of Christianity and is a historical result whenever Christ becomes an influence in the hearts of individuals. This change in the standard of living, however, should come through the national church and not be imposed by foreign missionaries. Ideally, the only time financial assistance for an improved standard of living should be given to Christians in foreign lands is when the standard has been lowered below normal for that area by unusual circumstances (flood, famine, etc.).

"The gospel of salvation is effective in changing any people on any level of civilization.[2] The duty of the missionary is not primarily to introduce higher standards of living . . . (but) to preach the gospel and assist in building the church. . . . Satan is very eager to throw a smoke screen or fog around the whole missionary process in an effort to get the missionary and the new Christians to dissipate their energies in an effort to change the physical aspects found in the mode of living.

"The reason we are so interested in missions is not only because Christ has commanded us to 'go into all the world' but [also] because we have realized the value of a soul. We know it does not profit if a man gains the whole world and loses his own soul. For this reason we are interested in evangelism. . . . When, through the Holy Spirit's leadership, this is accomplished, it not only gives peace in the midst of existing conditions, but often also gives an individual a desire to better his social conditions. It would seem that those who hold to indigenous principles are as much in favor of securing the social benefits of the gospel as any other Christian group, with this modification: the supporters of indigenous work believe that these benefits, the care of the widows and orphans, the healing of the sick, the education and training of the Christian constituency, should come through the church instead *Social Benefits through the Church* of through the missionary. Initial organizational plans and leadership may come from the missionary, but ideally the material support should come from the local church and its environment. This is the indigenous method, the New Testament way. To allow foreign material resources to underwrite these features of the local church program is to weaken the church. It will stunt its growth. . . . Between those who can think and work only for social betterment in foreign lands and those whose missionary work is only for the salvation of souls are those who have the concept of saving souls in order that the national Christian church may be established; which, in turn, will become the 'salt of the earth' and implement the social blessing of the Christian church. Anything that does not assist in establishing the church of Christ should be discouraged. Anything which hinders the development of the Church, no matter how much immediate good it does, should be sacrificed for the slower but more permanent good achieved through the establishment of the indigenous church.

"By assisting the nationals to better their conditions with American funds and plans, there is always the danger of confusing the minds of

*Confusing the Converts*

the nationals as to what Christianity really is. In the minds of these Christians, the gospel message, with its emphasis on salvation, becomes mixed with the material byproducts of the gospel. . . .

"It is quite apparent that whether it is in Africa, South America, or Asia, the people react in much the same way. They begin to expect material help wherever and whenever they can. . . . When we analyze the psychological results of free [medicine], free schooling, and free supplies upon the Christians, we soon find the 'rice Christian' psychology manifesting itself. The people, being very human, naturally gravitate to the mission where they can receive these material helps. When the material help is not forthcoming, then the individual missionary begins to sense a definite loss in their interest in his services. Some of these people . . . are very frank and remark: 'What is the use of being a Christian if we do not receive these benefits?' It is then that we begin to realize that these things which we thought would help the people have only hindered and confused them. The gospel message and its intent have been confused with the benefits which we thought were so essential as an outward expression of our concept of the gospel. . . . The people have unconsciously joined the group who followed

Jesus because they thought He would be King and provide them with food. . . . Eventually a clear-thinking missionary begins to realize that these benefits must be foregone if he is to get the true message of salvation and Jesus' purpose in coming to this world across to these people who have lived in heathen darkness and idolatrous practices.

"Is there a place for social service by the missionary? Yes, as an individual, the missionary will always be helping in social service activities, donating money from his personal funds, ministering to the sick, etc., but he will refrain from using missions funds. He will, as a Christian, administer the 'cup of cold water' in Christ's name, but as a missionary he will concentrate his energy, time, and foreign resources on the main task of planting the church."[3]

4. The missionary's ability and efficiency may prove to be a hindrance to the church's development. Impatient to attain certain goals, the missionary may use the direct approach instead of the slower, indirect way of working through the nationals. Americans are noted for their ability to get things *Want Quick Results?* done. Psychologically, we are geared to the machine age. *Fast* and *big* are words that occur frequently in our speech. "Within the boundaries of our evangelical standards, anything that produces results more rapidly is looked upon with favor, even though the permanent results may not be as satisfactory as (those) that might be obtained from other methods."[4]

Often we establish systems and a tempo that are beyond the capacity of the national and do not fit his nature. He observes the way the missionary does things, knows that he cannot do them in that way, and becomes discouraged. He cannot understand the American system of bookkeeping. He cannot carry through a complicated program that requires coordination of several diverse activities. The missionary may be a gifted musician and insist on the use of beautiful hymns. Perhaps under his guidance the believers learned to sing hymns with piano accompaniment. When the missionary leaves, the believers miss the piano, and their efforts to sing lack luster. Wouldn't it be better to allow them to accompany their hymns on a one-stringed instrument with which they are familiar and can continue to use when the missionary is not present?

Sometimes the missionary is too capable for the good of the national church. He does too much and sets a pace that is too fast. Believers watch him—not without admiration—and decide that since he does things so well, he should keep doing them.

Someone illustrated this point by asking how we would feel if we were placed with a group of illusionists. By trying to copy their actions, we certainly would end up feeling frustrated, bewildered, and discouraged. We don't have training to fit us for the task. Similarly, the quick, efficient Americans are like illusionists to the nationals. It is futile to try to force them into our pattern. We only discourage them. Rather, the missionary needs to educate himself and change his ways so that he follows the natural pattern of the nationals. We should not make the pattern of the work so foreign that it requires a foreign education to accomplish it.

An example is the missionary who is unwilling to wait for a national church to find the resources and make the effort to build a church. He knows that he can appeal to friends at home and receive more in one month than the church will raise in a year. His desire to "have something to show" for his labors may cause him to put aside the efforts of the nationals and build the church with outside funds.

Another missionary feels that he should continue to pastor the church where he resides, because no national worker is "big enough" for the central church. Better crowds attend when the missionary preaches, and he is somewhat impatient with the slow, easy approach of the national workers.

In both cases, following nonindigenous practices seem to produce more immediate results. However, the permanent results are far more discouraging. And these permanent results, which remain after the missionary is gone, are the true test of his labors.

## Rethink This Chapter

1. What conditions result when a missionary is unwilling to surrender his authority?

2. Why are some missionaries tempted to follow nonindigenous methods?

3. How might a missionary's honest desire to show Christian charity hinder him from attaining his true goal?

4. How has Christian charity sometimes produced a wrong mindset among nationals?

5. Since Christianity should bring social betterment, how can this be accomplished without weakening the moral fiber of national believers?

6. How can social service be accomplished without hindering the establishment of the indigenous church?

7. How does the efficiency and ability of the missionary sometimes discourage national initiative?

8. How can the missionary's desire to see big results in a short time hinder development of the indigenous church?

## Endnotes

[1] John Ritchie, *Indigenous Church Principles in Theory and Practice* (New York: Fleming H. Revell, 1946).

[2] For further comment see *Salvation Independent of Economic Conditions* (New York: World Dominion Movement).

[3] Based on information from the paper, "A Study of Indigenous Policies and Procedures," published by the Conservative Baptist Foreign Missions Society.

[4] Ibid.

# 10

# Relationship of the Missionary to the Indigenous Church

The missionary's ability to adjust to his environment and maintain a relationship with the church he plants has a major influence on the success of his labors. This chapter deals with a few problems in this area, followed by a summary of the missionary's proper ministry.

The first problem involves physical adjustment to the national environment, both in the home and in life. Someone once described a missionary as someone "called to cross national and cultural barriers which separate the peoples of this world. He is the 'apostle to the Gentiles,' a calling that necessitates a break with his own people and the adoption of a new home in a strange land. But the mere fact that a person leaves his native land for a foreign shore is no indication that the national and cultural barriers are crossed. The missionary frequently fails to make the break. He takes America with him. He establishes a small colony [and makes] . . . no effort to adopt the ways of the country as we would expect a guest to adjust his life in the home of a friend."

*Adjustment to Environment*

A consecrated national worker made this observation: "It pains us to see that some of our excellent missionaries have so little appeal to the people. This is because they live a life out of all proportion to their environment."

We make no plea for missionaries to adopt the national lifestyle. As a general rule, nationals expect missionaries to live differently. In some areas, it would be almost physically impossible for a missionary family to adjust to national foods and housing conditions. Even under the best conditions, missionaries suffer breakdowns in health because of diseases common to their new environment and changes in climate and food. Most missionaries find it necessary either to live on a higher scale than the nationals or to discontinue missionary work. Furthermore, the missionary's children need to live in an atmosphere that will familiarize them with American culture so they will not be misfits when they return to the States. For these reasons, missionaries must sometimes live on a scale that is beyond the reach of the average national.

Nevertheless, in the eyes of the nationals, missionaries—even those who reside in modest surroundings according to American standards—live like kings. The missionary family spends as much for one day's food as many nationals spend to feed an equal number of people for nearly a week. Missionaries may nonchalantly spend the equivalent of an average worker's monthly wage for an item that appears to be a nonessential trinket. Thus missionaries are considered "rich," and to protest otherwise is useless.

This discrepancy is a source of vexation to national Christians—especially national workers—who struggle in life. Conscientious missionaries also become distressed, and some of them will allow their sympathy to cloud their judgment. They begin to hand out financial gifts to others and start down the road toward the very thing they wanted to avoid—a church or worker financially dependent upon the mission. The missionary should remember that the worker is probably no worse off financially than he was before he accepted Christ, despite his current struggles. He is likely better off than those who are still without Christ. On the other hand, the missionary should endeavor to live as simply as possible and make no more show of money than is absolutely necessary. Explaining that equipment such as a refrigerator and car were made possible by sacrificial gifts from friends who desire to help him and his family spread the gospel may help give the national the right perspective.

What about the use of transportation and equipment such as power saws, electric lights and public-address systems? One mission board handled the question this way: "Indigenous methods, strictly applied, would rule out these modern factors if they were beyond the mechanical and technological level of the people we are trying to reach. If nationals could not carry on with these modern things without the help of [missionaries], and if they could not afford to buy these things if they had to be replaced, then there is a doubt as to the advisability of their use. It can just as logically be argued that the using of these modern things increases the effectiveness of the missionary one thousand percent. Both arguments are logical and right. *Modern Equipment* This illustration may throw a bit of light on the problem: A good father can do a certain job better and faster than his son, but he lets his son do it in order to teach him. He is preparing the son for the day when he will be on his own. He will not train the son with tools which the son himself cannot have later in life.

> From this illustration we may draw the general conclusion which may answer both logical arguments expressed above: As far as possible, . . . the missionary should use the transportation and mechanical developments used by the people. This is one phase of "reaching them on their own level." Where the missionary, after prayer and consideration, feels that the advantages gained by using modern things more than offset the disadvantages, he should use them only for personal use and not try to integrate them into the indigenous church. (Illustration: use a saw mill and a truck to build, but do not give the saw and the truck to the national church.) . . . Through all of this it should be kept in mind that spiritual concepts taught (and absorbed) are far more important and lasting than any material progress made. . . . Even though the nationals may greatly desire the foreign aid, we must carefully evaluate whether or not it will weaken the recipients.[1]

A second problem—financial relationships between the missionary with the indigenous church and the wrong use of foreign funds—has already been addressed. So what is the legitimate use of outside funds beyond the missionary's personal support and expenses?

> Of course missionaries and missions should not be [stingy]. There is a wise and loving use of money which opens the very gates of heaven to many a soul. But on mission fields, as at home, it is easy to . . . [misinterpret] a warm, sacrificial love of Christ and love for the people which would pour itself out for them without thought of remuneration, . . . [and respond with] a calculating, selfish attitude which demands so much pay for so much work. Indeed, every missionary society at home ought to make sure that its money is not used to the detriment of that which it would build up.
>
> Although a missionary must be extremely careful in the use of money, nevertheless he must show the people that it has cost him something to bring the gospel to them. Financial gifts rarely impress [national] Christians as involving any real sacrifice. On many fields the people in general think that all foreigners, Americans especially, are rich, and Christians share these views. It is in this connection that actual physical hardship and suffering speak to foreign peoples more eloquently than does the sacrifice of position, loved ones, or native land. Indeed, I have seen a pair of blistered feet do more for the advancement of the gospel than had gifts of hundreds of dollars by the missionary who owned those feet.
>
> This principle carries all the way through. Though one may deny a plea for funds with which to build a church, if he will sit down and help a congregation to figure out ways and means of building that church, if he will help them with his own hands, the people will see that he is actually giving in a way that costs. To sum it up, one might

*Limited Use of Foreign Funds*

say that the missionary should do only those things which the young church is unable to do for itself, not the things it is unwilling to do. And he should make certain that he does not decide too quickly, too unwisely, that a church is actually unable to do any task whatever that faces it.[2]

As a general policy, outside funds are best invested in aspects of the work that are beyond the reach of local churches and that serve to advance the work in the district, rather than the local church. Such use of foreign money can be a blessing as long as it does not build dependence upon those funds or substitute the nationals' effort with our own and cripple any initiative. We are to help churches do things, not do things for them.

A project that hastens the evangelization of a new district or a Bible school to train national workers both merit the wise investment of funds. Yet those funds should not be used in a way that causes churches and students to expect the mission to carry the financial burden for them. Investment in a tract of land to raise food for the Bible school—under the national church's supervision—could well pay rich dividends and help to make the Bible school self-supporting. The missionary must always think in terms of a self-supporting work and initiate each department of the work in such a way that the nationals can carry on after he is gone. He should refrain from starting anything that the nationals themselves cannot maintain.

These points summarize the missionary's ministry to the indigenous church:

a. The missionary is primarily a church planter. This work includes two phases—evangelizing the spiritually lost, teaching believers, and training national workers and leaders.

*Missionary's Ministry Summarized*

b. The missionary is a temporary factor in any local area. He should build the church in such a way that it can continue after he is gone. He should make the church—not himself—the primary source of ministry.

c. Since the missionary is a temporary factor, he should not allow himself to become bogged down with the routine of maintaining the work. Instead he must seek to occupy new fields. He cannot expect every detail of evangelism and organization to be worked out perfectly before he relinquishes direct oversight.

d. If the missionary finds an indigenous work already under way in his area—through spontaneous national effort or the fruit of missionary labors—he must be extremely careful not to adopt measures that will choke it. Missionaries eager to get such works under the mission's control can easily stifle them. A missionary might be tempted to pay a salary to the leader of the work. Later this leader may be content doing only a small part compared to what he previously did without financial assistance.

e. The missionary should refuse to occupy a position that a national can fill. He should avoid becoming tied down to a local pastorate and remain free to extend the work. He should count it a triumph when he is able to transfer responsibilities to national leaders.

f. The missionary should not jealously guard his own authority or position, but willingly let others take the lead. He should earn his position of leadership in the national church on the merits of his character and ministry. He must not feel that he merits a position of authority because he is a missionary. If leaders within the national church can fill offices in the work, the missionary should insist that they do so. The missionary's spiritual ministry will determine his proper place in the body of Christ and whether he holds an office.

g. Missionaries face a danger of leaving a work too soon. But a danger also exists in failing to leave at the proper time. When a missionary leaves the field before he has provided for vital teaching and

*Time of Withdrawl* leadership, the church is subject to the dangers of error and fanaticism. Believers may lapse back into their old ways, and the church disintegrate. These dangers can be avoided by following the Pauline example. The apostle Paul did not leave the churches he planted without instruction or leadership. The missionary must do more than gather a group of believers; he must incorporate them into a church under the guidance of the Holy Spirit.

On the other hand, failure to leave at the proper time breeds discontent and dwarfs the leadership of national believers. The missionary remains in one district when he could move on to a fruitful pioneer ministry.

After the missionary has turned over his responsibilities to national church leaders, he may still serve the church by placing himself at its disposal. He may be asked to help train national workers in the Bible school or push an aggressive evangelization program in some unreached area of the district. At the same time he will strengthen the new administration with his counsel. When the national leadership is sufficient to guide the churches, teach new workers in the Bible school, and initiate progressive evangelism efforts in the main areas of the district, then the missionary's work there is finished. With a grateful heart he can move to a neighboring district or transfer to a new field to begin planting churches again.

No other aspect will influence the indigenous church more than the missionary's approach to spiritual leadership. Above everything else, he must be a spiritual example to believers and workers, a man who can prevail with God and prepare the way for the moving of the Holy Spirit. It is sad when national believers outstrip the missionary

## The Missionary's Spiritual Leadership

in spiritual vision. They look to the missionary not merely for his organizational ability and Bible knowledge but also for leadership and inspiration. When these qualities are not evident, they have to go on without him. Above all else, let the missionary maintain his standing as a man of God. In doing so, all other relationships will be much easier to cultivate.

## Rethink This Chapter

1. What problem does the missionary face in adjusting to the national environment?
2. Should a missionary totally adopt the national lifestyle in order to win people?
3. Why are ordinary Americans considered rich by nationals?
4. What arguments are made both for and against the use of modern equipment in missions work?

5. What policy should guide missionaries regarding whether to use modern equipment?

6. How can a missionary help the national church without making a financial gift?

7. How are outside funds best used to help the work on a particular field?

8. How do missionaries tend to sacrifice mobility for the sake of maintaining an established work?

9. What temptation besets the missionary when he finds a spontaneous effort under way in his area?

10. What attitude should the missionary take concerning his own ministry and his assumption of official posts in the national church?

11. What is the danger of leaving a work prematurely?

12. What is the danger of staying with a work too long?

13. When is a missionary's work done in a given district?

14. In what way does a missionary make the greatest impression for good upon the national church?

## Endnotes

[1] From a paper, "A Study of Indigenous Policies and Procedures," published by the Conservative Baptist Foreign Missions Society.

[2] The Independent Board bulletin.

# 11

# Pentecost and Indigenous Methods

Spiritual awakenings and revivals can be lost if proper methods are not used to harness and conserve the results. This is one reason why indigenous methods are so important. A great revival can die out or become ineffective if a scriptural course toward New Testament goals is not applied. Even the best methods will produce nothing unless they are accompanied by the Holy Spirit's work. As a well-tuned motor needs gasoline and a spark to operate, the church needs indigenous principles and spiritual power to be strong and effective. New Testament methods are the mechanics of a successful church on the mission field; the power and ministries of the Holy Spirit provide the dynamics. Either factor alone is incomplete and inadequate.

After trying indigenous methods, some missionaries report that the work reached a certain stage and then failed to progress. They use this as an argument against indigenous principles. Since believers lacked initiative and the churches barely held their own, the missionaries conclude that the nationals simply are not up to an aggressive program and will lapse into inertia if left to themselves. Therefore, missionaries must be on hand constantly to inspire and direct if the church is to make progress.

The trouble is not in the indigenous principles, for these are the New Testament methods. The difficulty may be that the indigenous methods are only partially or imperfectly applied. On the other hand, they may be applied but are not accompanied by New Testament power. New Testament Christians received such an enduement of power and inflow of divine life that their doubts, fears, and inertia were swept aside. "Wherever they went," they testified of Christ's resurrection (Acts 8:4). We may set up the perfect "mechanism" of an indigenous church, but without the divine "combustible" of the Holy Spirit's power, it will be ineffective.

The genius of the Pentecostal movement is uniquely suited to the indigenous church method. Thousands of indigenous churches sprang into existence as a result of Pentecostal outpourings. These outpourings always produced believers with flaming zeal and a sacrificial spirit.

The emphasis on each believer's need to receive a personal infilling of the Holy Spirit produces believers and workers of unusual zeal and power. Emphasizing the present-day working of miracles and healing awakens whole communities and convinces unbelievers of the power of

*Pentecost Uniquely Suited*

God. People see a power at work that is superior to that of their witch doctors and spiritual leaders. Pentecostals have faith in the Holy Spirit's ability to give spiritual gifts and supernatural abilities to the common people, including those who might be termed "unlearned." They believe a host of lay preachers and leaders of unusual spiritual ability—not unlike the rugged fishermen who first followed the Lord—can be raised up.

We have witnessed the miracle of transformation that the Holy Spirit's presence produces in a national church. Lethargic and reluctant workers are transformed into zealous witnesses willing to launch out into new towns and villages without any promise of support. Suspicious, sensitive, and squabbling believers join together in divine love to become a powerful force for the kingdom of God.

A vital turning point took place in Central America after seventy-five believers—including several workers—were filled with the Holy Spirit in one week. In the following eighteen months about three hundred people received the fullness of the Spirit. Within two years from the first blessing, the number of workers, churches, and believers practically doubled. Soon the gospel was preached in areas that would have remained unreached for many years under ordinary circumstances.

To be successful in indigenous church ministry, missionaries do more than teach and initiate believers in right methods. They must also introduce believers into the realm of the Holy Spirit's workings. New Testament methods coupled with New Testament power is the answer to present-day problems on the mission

*Producing the Power*

field. Let the missionaries of each field gather to pray until a spiritual awakening takes place according to the apostolic pattern. Include national believers in this prayer ministry for revival. Both missionaries and national church leaders should not only preach a gospel of power, but also pray until they catch the flame in their own hearts. We cannot expend more energy then we receive from our Source. Individually and collectively, we must give time to this most important of all ministries—praying until God's blessings are outpoured. Then we can use New Testament methods to funnel these blessings toward building a vigorous national church. This kind of ministry justifies the presence of the missionary on foreign soil and gives him a rightful claim to the noble title of "Church Builder."

> Jesus said: "I will build my church, and the gates of Hades will not overcome it" (Matthew 16:18).

> "Then the disciples went out and preached everywhere, and the Lord worked with them and confirmed his word by the signs that accompanied it" (Mark 16:20).

## Rethink This Chapter

1. What is the difference between the mechanics and the dynamics of the indigenous church?
2. What are two reasons why indigenous methods have failed in some areas?
3. Why is the "genius of the Pentecostal movement uniquely suited to the indigenous church method"?

4. How do Pentecostal teachings on the baptism in the Holy Spirit, divine healing, and the gifts of the Spirit contribute to the development of the indigenous church?

5. What steps taken by the missionary will help bring the Holy Spirit's divine power into operation in the national church?

*Book Two:*

# The Indigenous Church and the Missionary

# Preface to the First Edition

The author's book *The Indigenous Church* was first published in 1953. It was originally written for the purpose of offering assistance to the author's coworkers on the mission field, particularly those connected with his own mission. The reception that this book enjoyed was far greater than anticipated, and a companion book, *Build My Church*, was produced that was intended to help national church leaders. This latter book also had wide acceptance around the world and has been translated into more than a dozen languages.

*The Indigenous Church* was republished by Moody Press under the title *On the Mission Field: The Indigenous Church*, and at a still later date after some revision, it was given a new title, *Growing Young Churches*.

More than twenty years have passed since *The Indigenous Church* was first published. Missionary co-laborers have suggested that now since indigenous churches are functioning in most of the countries in which we labor, something should be written to missionaries in their present situation. Thank God the national church has developed with its own officers and organizational structure. Of necessity, the role of the missionary has changed as the national church has come into its own.

To give some assistance to those who are already in missionary work and to those missionary candidates who are going to the field for the first time, this little volume, *The Indigenous Church and the Missionary*, is offered. In this volume the author attempts to deal with the problems the new situation has produced. However, the scope of the book is not limited to the solving of problems, but attempts to show the opportunities for ministry that exist in working in partnership with the national church and gives some guidelines as to how this task may be approached.

It is the author's hope that this effort will prove a blessing to those engaged in missionary labors.

Melvin L. Hodges, 1978

# 1

# The Church's Mission to Today's World

The terms *missions* and *missionary* are likely to bring widely differing mental images to different persons. Some will envision immediately a man in a pith helmet about to be devoured by cannibals. Some may see the same type of individual endeavoring to teach a group of naked children to read. Others will picture an austere spinster completely absorbed in civilizing and clothing primitive tribes. Still others see the missionary as a "do-gooder" engaged in philanthropic efforts of educational or medical institutions, striving to bring relief and betterment to underprivileged peoples. And then there are those who view the missionary as an anthropological nuisance who unnecessarily introduces changes into the cultural life of the noble and contented savage.

All such concepts, while perhaps having their roots in some real-life situations, nevertheless fail to include the one basic and essential element of missions. The missionary is above everything else a proclaimer of the good news of the kingdom of God.

In the first century of the Christian church, the Christian mission was not identifiable in terms of a wealthy nation taking material benefits to an underdeveloped people. Probably the people of Macedonia and Asia Minor were not underprivileged economically or culturally in relation to the sending churches of Antioch or Jerusalem. The mission of the apostles was to share the riches of the gospel of Jesus Christ with those who did not have this knowledge. Today, the cultural and economical facets of missions usually loom larger in the minds of the general public than does the spiritual task of the messenger of Jesus Christ. This confusion in the minds of the people, and often in the minds of missionaries themselves, has often dulled the sharp cutting edge of Christian missions.

We could well wish that the situation were different and that Christian missions could be defined simply as taking the gospel of Jesus Christ to people that did not have this knowledge. But like it or not, the mission of the evangelical church today is judged in the light of political and economic factors rather than evaluated solely on the basis of the message that the missionary brings. Nevertheless, we reaffirm that in a biblical sense, mission is not to be confused with cultural or economic factors but is rather the activity of those who know Jesus Christ simply sharing this knowledge with those who do not know Him.

The situation of the underdeveloped countries, especially since World War II, has radically changed. Radio, roads, and the airplane have all contributed to a communication explosion that has brought these areas closer to the rest of the world. Education is of highest priority. The development of national resources, the introduction of manufacturing, and increased traffic in commerce have all had their profound effect.

In the short span of the writer's own missionary experience he has witnessed the effect of industrialization of far-removed places and peoples: a road opening up a new section of a country so that in two hours by car one can travel the distance that formerly required two days by horse; a transistor radio on the backpack of a Bolivian Highland Indian, providing music and bringing him into contact with the larger world, as he himself climbs laboriously the steep Andean road; crowds of people, young and old, thronging the streets of a large city at 10 p.m. as night schools finish another day of classes in adult education—all these are pungent indications of the changes that are taking place in underdeveloped countries.

Probably one of the greatest single factors is the emerging of former colonies as sovereign nations. Among these people, national pride runs high. These nations are no longer willing to meekly follow the leadership of the politically and economically more advanced nations. They want to occupy in their own right their place as a nation under the sun. Even in Latin America, where colonial domination has generally not been practiced since these nations overthrew the yoke of Spain and Portugal, the thrust for national identity is a powerful force. The United States is castigated for its "economic colonialism," and nationalism often finds expression in anti-Yankee speeches and slogans.

## Changes Affect Missionary Activity

All this could not but affect the position of the missionary from economically developed countries as he seeks to carry on his spiritual ministry. In those countries that were previously colonies of powerful nations, the missionary, because of his own nationality and race, was automatically identified with colonial rule. Often, if he had any difficulties with the local government, he could depend upon the help and backing from the colonial authorities. In Latin America, it was commonly the case that the U.S. citizen, including the missionary, was given preferential treatment. He was often served first in the store and in public office before others who had arrived before him. He was representative of the great and powerful country to the north; he was considered to be better educated, to have more know-how, and to be in many ways superior to the local population. All this has changed rapidly since World War II. Quite often the North American finds that he is the last one to go through immigrations and customs as he enters a country. His nationality, far from making him popular and respected by the local populous, may often prove to be a hindrance to him in establishing good relations.

## The Missionary and the National Church

There is another element of change that particularly affects the missionary, and this is the development of the overseas church. When the pioneer missionaries went out, they found themselves alone and without a Christian community. Their principal work was that of evangelism and hopefully the establishing of a church. The missionary, as pioneer, was the "father" of the work. He was respected, and often his leadership and decisions were followed without question. In the course of time, by the grace of God, a national church developed. The work grew from three to five or ten churches, and finally some kind of a council or conference was formed. In the beginning, usually the missionary filled a prominent place in the infant church organization.

As the church spread and the national organization became stronger, national ministers began to fill the executive positions and the missionary was no longer the chief executive of the church. In the meantime, other missionaries reached the field to pioneer new areas or teach in Bible institutes and otherwise help to develop the national church. These were not the original pioneers and did not enjoy the same prestige that the pioneers did. Further, in some cases, the national pastors often actually had more preaching and administrative experience than did the new missionary. So today the younger missionary must find his role in the work on a different basis than did the pioneer. Probably 90 percent of missionaries going to the foreign field today find their place alongside of comparatively mature national workers and contribute to an already established church.

It is in this changed world that today's missionary must fulfill God's call. He must understand the role which he is to play in the great drama of church development. If he fails to adjust to these new conditions, he will become frustrated and defeated. If he can learn to accept the new situations and work with them, he has before him a door of unparalleled opportunity and response.

## *The Missionary Task Today*

Faced with these circumstances, many questions arise. What is the true role of today's missionary? What is the missionary task? On what basis should rich America share its financial resources with the undeveloped church overseas?

It is apparent that it becomes a missionary's responsibility to separate the passing from the permanent. He must distinguish between the changing and the changeless. He is called upon to adapt his methods to the requirements of changing times, while at the same time he must never truncate his message by surrendering eternal truths or principles for the sake of expediency.

The Great Commission rests upon the authority of our living Lord and upon His command to preach the gospel to every creature, and it will retain its imperative as long as there are lost men without the knowledge of Christ. The role of the missionary is primarily that of evangelist, church planter, and church developer. He may on occasion find it necessary to fill administrative posts related to the maintenance of the established churches. He may find that circumstances require him to engage temporarily in secular education or do translation work. All of these things he may do as necessity dictates, but he ought not lose sight of the fact that his essential calling—his reason for being a missionary—is evangelism, church planting, and development.

The church that the missionary plants on the mission field ought to be of the same spiritual quality as that of the true Church anywhere and in all ages. The church overseas should share the vitality of the New Testament Church. This signifies that it must accept the responsibility of being a church. This responsibility includes the developing of its own spiritual resources for propagating the gospel to its own people. It means finding the financial and material resources necessary for maintaining and expanding the work. It requires that the church overseas develop to become responsible for its own decisions under the leadership of the Holy Spirit and in accordance with the Word of God. These factors are innate in a truly New Testament church. The missionary's contribution is primarily that of founding and contributing to the development of this kind of church.

# 2

# New Testament Missions Are Church-Oriented Missions

The Church today in general suffers from a weak theology of mission. Mission, in turn, suffers from a weak theology of the Church. Actually, church and mission are two halves of a whole. Mission is the Church in action. The Church in turn is the product of biblical missions. We only deceive ourselves and abort God's purpose when we think of the Church in something other than New Testament terms and of the Christian mission as something other than the New Testament mandate.

Biblically, we must consider at least two main aspects of the Church, and there is the suggestion of a third. There is the Church mystical and universal, made up of all true believers in the Lord Jesus Christ, regardless of their race or church affiliation. Then, there are local churches in different cities and communities with their elders, deacons, and members. There is also a suggestion of churches as national or regional units which represent the community of local churches in a given region, such as "the churches of Judea" and the "churches of Asia." In this concept the many local churches in different localities become "the church" of the nation or region (1 Corinthians 16:19; 2 Corinthians 8:1; 1 Thessalonians 2:14).

Geography, language, and political barriers cause the churches to fall into different groups. The churches brought into existence upon an island would have a different relationship to each other in the same locality than they would to churches in some distant land who might be totally unknown to them. Denominational churches, of course, were unknown in the New Testament.

## The Church Is of Intrinsic Value to God

The New Testament shows that God has a special plan and purpose for the Church, both because of what it is to Him and because of its mission to the world. In that first church council at Jerusalem, James declared that God did visit the Gentiles "to take out of them a people for his name" (Acts 15:14, KJV). This people became "a chosen people, a royal priesthood, a holy nation, a people belonging to God" (1 Peter 2:9). The apostle Paul declared that this Church is to become the bride of Christ (Ephesians 5:23–32; see also Revelation 19:7–9).

The Church then has a special relationship to God and to the Lord Jesus Christ. Jesus loved it and gave himself for it (Ephesians 5:25). This tells of the love of God for the Church for its own sake, both in time and eternity.

## The Church Is God's Instrument for Evangelism

At the same time, the Church is not only a "pearl of great price" for which the Redeemer gave His all, but the Church, while in the world, is God's instrument for the fulfilling of His eternal purpose in the world. Again, Peter reminds us of our mission to the world, "that you may declare the praises of him who called you out of darkness into his wonderful light" (1 Peter 2:9).

It was to the Church "in embryo" that Jesus said, "Therefore go and make disciples of all nations, baptizing them in the name of the Father and of the Son and of the Holy Spirit, and teaching them to obey everything I have commanded you. And surely I am with you always, to the very end of the age" (Matthew 28:19,20). Luke records Christ's words, "But you will receive power when the Holy Spirit comes on you; and you will be my witnesses in Jerusalem, and in all Judea and Samaria, and to the ends of the earth" (Acts 1:8).

So the Church is called to be an instrument for evangelism: to proclaim the good news, nurture converts, and build itself up, both locally and universally: "From him the whole body, joined and held together by every supporting ligament, grows and builds itself up in love, as each part does its work" (Ephesians 4:16). This then is the Church's responsibility and mission. The fact that we are living in the twentieth century rather than in the first does not alter the commission. Let us therefore explore the mission of the Church to the modern world.

## The Nature of the Church's Mission

The Church's mission is a witness to individuals. "Go into all the world and preach the good news to all creation" (Mark 16:15). Every soul has a right to hear the gospel proclaimed by God through Jesus Christ, His Son. As long as one soul exists that has not had this opportunity, the mission of the Church is unfulfilled.

The Church, however, is more than scattered individual believers in Jesus Christ. It is a corporate body (1 Corinthians 12:13). It is a holy nation; a special people (1 Peter 2:9,10). It is an assembly and congregation (Hebrews 10:25). The work of evangelism is not completed until individual believers can be formed into a local church, which in turn will become God's agent for spreading the good news of the gospel.

The Christian mission today has often been weakened and sidetracked from its original purpose. Present-day substitutions for Christian missions are confusing the issues in many sections of the Christian church. Social and political action are being called for instead of the effort to convert men to faith in Christ. Some say that the call to individual repentance is no longer pertinent—that it is rather society that must repent, since it is the present oppressive society with its inhumanity to man that produces an ever-increasing harvest of oppressed individuals who turn to vice and crime. Converting one individual, they claim, is of little value as long as the system produces them by the thousands. We are told that we should not call men to become members of Christ's Church, since this separates them from their own people and culture. The argument here is that the church removes people from society and builds a wall between them and the world when the need is for men who will become incarnate in the world and work for a new social system. Traditional Christian terms such as "evangelism," "reconciliation," "repentance," and "conversion" are used with new meanings to apply to this concept of social activism.

What is the Christian mission? Is it a benevolent attempt to better social and economic conditions in the world or an attempt to exercise political influence and power?

The term "Christian missions" has fallen into disrepute in some circles as an anachronism. The more popular term today is "Christian mission." Missions refers to the now outdated (they say) concept that the Church must preach the gospel to individuals and establish churches. The Church is in the world as God's mission, and this concept must not be limited to preaching the gospel to the heathen but should be applied to the whole of man and his life. The geographical barriers are blurred between the sending church and the receiving church. The church must think of mission in six continents. At the same time, the distinction between the Church and the world is blurred. The Church is mission, we are told. Everything the Church does is mission. Sometimes the Church fulfills its mission simply by maintaining the Christian presence in a given area or situation.

Certainly there is no quarrel with the idea that everything that Christians are and do should contribute to the growth of the kingdom of God, and we happily agree that a true Christian presence, the living out of the gospel of Christ, is indispensable. But we do strenuously object to the idea that everything Christians do (honest toil and voting) is per se the fulfilling of the Great Commission. The fact that the Christian presence witnesses to the grace of God is not reason to omit or find unnecessary the vigorous proclamation of the good news. Whatever term is employed, the biblical interpretation of the Christian mission requires the emphasis of calling men from darkness to light, and the presentation of Jesus Christ as the only Savior.

Some are saying that the Church should lose itself in society—like a grain of wheat that falls into the ground to die, losing its identity, and merging with the political forces of revolution in order to bring about a secular "city of God."

James A. Scherer observes,

> It is suggested that Black Power, African and Latin American liberation movements might be taken as possible models in interpreting the current quest for salvation. The problem is that contemporary movements add little or nothing to the once-for-all given basis and foundation of the Christian mission in God's reconciling act in Jesus Christ. The motive and power for mission are not found in the questions and cries of the world, though from such questions and cries we can get valuable guidance for the direction and carrying out of our mission. Response to human need forms the catalyst, but it is never in itself the motive.[1]

Many examples exist of the misguided enthusiasm of certain church leaders toward a particular political movement, which they believed would benefit the country and the church, only to end up in disappointment. Man cannot foresee the future, and he underestimates the forces of corruption at work in the human heart. The answer to the world's needs will never be found in the plans and programs of unregenerate men. Let us remind ourselves of what happened to the Church and to the world in the middle ages when the Church attained political power.

In making these observations, we are not shutting our eyes to the injustices that exist in the world. We are simply stating that the mission of the Church is to preach the gospel of Jesus Christ, which will transform the hearts of men and women and make them new creatures with new desires and a transformed character. We believe this is the only hope for this world. The fact that the Christian faith has not yet brought about a complete transformation of society must be taken in the light of what the Scriptures teach about the course of events, i.e., that evil will increase in the world before the Kingdom comes in power. Also, the fact is that many who call themselves Christians are not necessarily reborn men. They are nominal Christians who have not experienced the transforming power of the gospel in their lives.

Basically, the Christian believer is "not of the world" (John 17:16). While God is not indifferent to politics, He has not chosen the political world as His medium of action in bringing to fruition the redemption of humanity. His chosen instrumentality is the Church. While God has a plan for this world, the Scriptures do not indicate that the Church should join arm in arm with ungodly and atheistic forces to bring about a remedy to cure its ills. Rather, His people will recognize the lordship of the Redeemer, place themselves in His hands to do His bidding in carrying His gospel to the ends of the earth, and thus be "the light of the world" and "the salt of the earth."

Again Scherer declares, "The Christian mission can include no less than the full Christological witness to salvation and grace in Jesus Christ. The suppression of the witness is unthinkable, for the name and power are inseparable."[2]

True Christianity calls for the intervention of God himself in the person of Jesus Christ in order to establish righteousness upon the earth. We must not confuse the biblical mission of the Church with the humanistic ideas of natural man.

The Church is to be planted in every land. We have already pointed out that the Church is to be an instrument for evangelism. This means that the Church that is to result from missionary effort must be the Church in the true sense of the word. It must be New Testament in doctrine, experience, and power. It is not enough to establish a branch of a Christian church that depends on the United States or Europe for the supplying of its needs. The Church must be the CHURCH, and the Church that is brought into existence through the proper preaching of the Word, through the power of the Holy Spirit, will have the basic characteristics of the New Testament Church. Something is amiss if we bring into existence a church that is weak, dependent, and without initiative.

It goes without saying that the Western world can never send enough missionaries to do the work of evangelism that is required to reach the multiplied millions who are yet without Christ. It is also an accepted fact that Western churches cannot produce enough workers or pastors to take care of the churches that will spring up. This means that the church that is raised up on the foreign field must be endued with the same missionary spirit as was the church that sent the missionary out to evangelize in the first place. Anything less will not meet the requirements of today's world. When the church is planted, it becomes the normal agency through which God will work to continue the task of total evangelism.

The stability and growth of a budding church requires that it be firmly established in the Word of God. Paul attributed the stability of the church in Thessalonica to the fact that the Word had penetrated the lives of the believers (1 Thessalonians 2:13; see also Acts 2:42). The teaching of the Word must be given to all believers, and not just to those who may become leaders, for the entire congregation needs to be well rooted in the truths of the gospel.

One of the most important factors in establishing a church is the development of national leadership. This leadership must be truly called of God and filled with the Spirit, for it is the Holy Spirit with His anointing and spiritual gifts who provides the indispensable preparation for the work of the ministry. Moreover, such men require training for their task. Without question, one of the greatest contributions of missions, outside of evangelism itself, is the developing of national leaders who can guide their people with blessing, wisdom, and power, not only into Christian maturity, but for the continuing of the task of total evangelism.

The church developed on the mission field shares also the missionary responsibility. It is not enough that the church be trained to maintain itself, but it must partake of the apostolic spirit and engage in evangelism of its own people and send out workers to the unevangelized even beyond its borders.

## Endnotes

[1] Sherer, James A. "Three Essentials in 'Salvation Today,'" *Evangelical Missions Quarterly*, Vol. 7, No. 4, Summer 1972.

[2] Ibid.

# 3

# The Missionary's Partnership with the Overseas Church

In the first chapter it was pointed out that the status of the missionary has been changed considerably due to the political and economic factors that have been at work these last decades. His relationship with the national church is on a different basis than was that of the pioneer missionary who arrived in the country to establish a church. These factors bring into sharp focus the necessity of the missionary to understand his present role.

## How Permanent Is the Missionary Ministry?

At this point, the question arises as to how permanent the ministry of a missionary is in a given area. In an earlier book, *The Indigenous Church* (1953), the author made the comparison of the ministry of the missionary to that of scaffolding on a building. The object, it was stated, is to build the building—which in this case is the church—and when the church is built, the scaffolding is taken down as it is not a part of the permanent structure. In this we have the example of the apostle Paul who founded the church in different cities and countries and then passed on to continue his ministry in other areas. He did not consider himself as a permanent part of any local church. This viewpoint has raised considerable objections on the part of some missionary leaders and national ministers. One African national church leader has stated that the African church wants missionaries who will put down their roots and give their lives for the church. They are not interested in a temporary ministry. It seems evident that both viewpoints have validity. It must be understood that two different emphases are in mind.

In comparing the missionary as scaffolding and using the familiar term that "the missionary should work himself out of a job," it should be remembered that the point of emphasis is that the missionary should develop national church leadership rather than consider himself the permanent leader of the church. Much has transpired since those viewpoints were expressed. At that time in some cases, missionaries were pastoring churches that had had missionary pastors for a whole generation, and there was still no national leader capable of taking over. Missionaries were often considered automatically to be the superintendents of the work. The statement that the missionary should consider himself as scaffolding of temporary usefulness was intended to emphasize the need of the missionary to plant a church that would be able to support itself, govern itself, and propagate itself. The New Testament example is strongly behind this viewpoint. The missionary's task is to mature the church and raise up the necessary leaders. Nationals should be pastors, should fill the national organization's official posts, and the time should come when national leaders should also become instructors and presidents of the Bible institutes. The church on the foreign field should be complete. It is an inadequate concept to maintain that any area of the church's life must permanently be supplied from a foreign country.

However, these concepts were never intended to convey the idea that the missionary had nothing left to offer the national church once a national leadership is developed. Paul strengthened the churches that he raised up by repeated visits and by writing letters to them. While the missionary may no longer be the superintendent of the national organization or pastor the principal churches, his ministry may still be required for the extension and maturing of the church in many different areas.

## *All Missionary Ministries Are Not the Same*

Actually all missionary ministries are not the same. Paul recognized this. To the Corinthian church he stated, "I planted the seed, Apollos watered it, but God made it grow" (1 Corinthians 3:6). Some missionaries have distinctive pioneer ministries for establishing the church. Others have a very important and essential ministry in "watering" the church. Paul left Titus in Crete for such a missionary ministry: to "straighten out what was left unfinished" (Titus 1:5). Timothy also evidently had such a "watering" ministry among the churches. He was left in Ephesus by Paul to strengthen that church which was troubled by false doctrines (1 Timothy 1:3,4).

Missionaries going out into the foreign field today will often find a national church already in existence. Pioneer missionaries who have planted the church in the beginning and are still on the field will rejoice that their ministry has been fruitful inasmuch as they have brought into existence a church that is able to govern itself and develop ministries that will edify and mature the church. Rather than feeling rejected, they should find this a cause for rejoicing.

As circumstances change, the Holy Spirit will also change the ministry of the missionaries to meet the different needs. Among the overseas churches there is a great need for teaching. Teaching in the Bible institutes or Bible colleges offers missionaries a challenging opportunity where some may well spend the rest of their years contributing to the development of the national leadership. There are also ministries of literature, radio, correspondence schools, and evangelistic campaigns. Often there are areas in the country where the church has not yet been planted and the missionary can return to his primary calling of a church planter.

## Tensions Resulting from Change

As could be expected, this change of roles on the part of a missionary and his relationship to the national church can be tension-producing.

Both the missionary and the national church may experience difficulty in finding the proper relationship to each other. The fact that a changed situation has produced tensions is acknowledged by all. As the national church reaches maturity, the missionary is no longer over the national church. Some mission boards have gone to the extreme of placing the missionary under the national church. In fact, the missionary is sometimes no longer called by that name. He is called a "fraternal worker." Even his finances may be handled through the national church, and he is assigned his task by the executives of the national organization.

Certainly, we agree that missionaries should have the spiritual maturity to serve under the national church if this would be required. The Bible tells us to submit ourselves one to another, for all of us to be clothed with humility. Without question, such arrangements give ample opportunities for the missionary to demonstrate Christian character in his humility and willingness to serve his brethren. Also, it demonstrates the truth that in Christ there are no racial distinctions. However, serious doubts do exist as to whether this procedure is really productive. Many problems and frustrations arise with this arrangement. It seems in part to be artificial, imposed on the missionary rather than growing out of his calling and ministry.

Two things must be kept in mind in considering this. In the first place, the missionary is sent to fulfill a ministry in which church planting and church maturing have priority. There is a distinct possibility that the national leaders may not have the same vision for the growth of the church, and that instead of producing greater church growth, making the missionary's assignment entirely subject to the national executives, they could actually hinder it. We have known of cases where, if the national organization or a superintendent had had his say, a missionary would have been placed as an assistant to a national pastor. Other missionaries have expressed concern that they might be removed from an evangelistic ministry and placed as supervisors of day schools. Some missionaries have found their situation so frustrating that they have left the field.

The missionary's personal call of God is involved in this matter. The Holy Spirit endows men with gifts for certain ministries, and we must not consent to an arrangement whereby the will of God is not permitted to find fruition because of arbitrary decisions.

## Missionary and National Church Relationships

The ideal situation is for the missionaries to enter into a partnership with the national church. Some mission groups have opted for a complete separation between the national church and the mission.

Missionaries in this case are not members of the national church and can hold no offices in the national church, but operate a parallel organization and meet in consultation with the leaders of the national church to offer the church certain services that the church still needs. This procedure is unavoidable where the missionary body is seeking to serve a national church that was established, perhaps by the national Christians themselves, previous to the coming of the missionary. The missionary did not grow up with the church, and now if he is to serve it, it must be by offering services the national church is not yet capable of performing. This could well take the form of providing literature or of establishing a Bible institute for the training of the national pastors of that group. Even so, the more integrated that he can become in brotherly love and confidence with the national church, the more fruitful his ministry will be.

Personally, I would favor integration of the missionary into the national church where this is possible. It seems to be beneficial for the missionary to be considered as a member of the national church while it is young and struggling toward maturity. For a time, the missionary can serve as a superintendent and show the way. The vision and energy of the missionary set an example for the church that is just learning to take its first steps. We have seen a national church stagnate because of having leaders who were not yet mature or experienced enough to lead a national organization.

When a national is placed as leader of the work before he has the experience and has developed his administrative gifts sufficiently, it sometimes happens that he depends on the missionary for guidance. This, of course, is helpful, but unfortunately this dependence often produces dissatisfaction among the pastors. They tend to see the leader as the missionary's man and may finally reject him as a puppet. In such cases, the missionary is still the actual leader of the work, and it would seem better for him to openly assume this responsibility until nationals are prepared to take it.

The danger, of course, in permitting missionaries to hold offices in the national church is that they may continue in such posts too long and consider themselves as the rightful leaders of the national church, rather than attempting to develop the leadership of the nationals themselves. However, where there is spiritual vision and understanding of the goals, it should not be difficult for missionaries to recognize the point at which they should not permit their names to be considered any longer for official posts so that the national brethren may occupy these positions.

However the details may be worked out, we believe that a partnership arrangement is ideal. The missionary is neither over nor under the national church, but working alongside the church as a fellow worker. It is interesting to note that Assemblies of God World Missions has tooled out the following statement to define this relationship.

> The missionary is the servant of the Lord in the implementation of the Great Commission and in every respect is to seek the enhancement of the national church. Missionary field councils or representatives shall, through dialogue and mutual agreement, seek to work together with the national church in the common cause of winning the lost and further establishing indigenous New Testament churches. It is understood that such cooperation implies neither absorption into nor exclusion, from the national church.
>
> The missionary must be flexible, for his role will change as the national church matures. The actual missionary-national relationship will be determined by the need for cooperation and unity in the mutual God-given responsibility for complete world evangelization. In so doing, the missionary must not abdicate his responsibility to world evangelism and church planting, neither by perpetuating the mission's authority over the national church nor by succumbing to nationalistic interests that would prevent him from fulfilling the Great Commission (*The Missionary Manual of the Assemblies of God*).

## Open Discussion

The question of a missionary's location and assignment requires open discussion and communication. In the placing of a missionary, the missionary organization should not have the total say, nor should the national church be the only voice that decides this question.

Three things are involved: first, the purpose of the missionary body in sending the missionary to the field; second, the desires of the national executives as they see the needs of the field; and third, the individual calling of the missionary himself. The missionary cannot do his best work if he does not feel that he is in the place where God wants him to serve. Therefore, these three factors should line up, not by arbitrary decisions of any one of the three, but by prayerful consultation. Since the Holy Spirit is in charge of the Church, this is not an impossible solution. God can guide so that the decision reached is satisfactory to all concerned.

## Recognition of National Church Authority

In the final analysis, of course, the national church is the official organization in the country, and the missionary is there by the consent of the foreign government and in a certain sense is a guest of the church. If matters reach an impasse, it is entirely possible that the national church would have final say with the government as to whether a visa could be granted. In such a case, the individual missionary will have to seek God to know how he should proceed if the decision of the national church is not in harmony with his own convictions. However, it is our experience that missionaries who have an anointed ministry, a godly Christian character, and humility enough to acknowledge the authority of the national church and work with it usually have no trouble in finding an open door. In fact, in spite of anti-missionary and anti-American sentiment, I have yet to see the national church close the doors to a missionary with an anointed ministry and a proper attitude toward his brethren.

# 4

# Establishing a Partnership with the National Church

We shall now examine the factors that must be taken into consideration in establishing a viable partnership with the national church. We are at present concerned with the missionary who works in a country where a national church has come into existence either through his own efforts or the efforts of others. All the executive officers of the church are now national brethren. The original pioneer effort of the missionary in getting the church started has been accomplished. The missionary, however, is staying on in the country to "water" the budding church and must enter into a working partnership with the church. He needs to find a place of fulfillment for his ministry where he can make a valuable contribution to the church and yet avoid tension-producing situations. Vergil Gerber states the situation succinctly in the following phrases: "Churches produced missions. Missions produced churches. Their success produced tensions."[1]

## Causes for Tensions

### Culturally Oriented Tensions

Many of the tensions that arise between missionaries and nationals are culturally oriented. While some of these things cannot be helped because of the differences in background, yet by being aware of their existence, the missionary can help to minimize them.

A frequent complaint against certain missionaries is the fact that they *do not speak the language well*. We have known of students in

Bible schools who complain that they do not understand what the missionary is trying to teach them. Perhaps it would not be going too far to state that many missionaries overestimate their ability in the language. They sometimes think that they speak better than they do. This is a constant challenge and requires continual effort. The missionary should not discontinue language study because he is able to carry on a conversation. He should study the language as long as he ministers to a people. Newspapers in the vernacular should be read along with books by native authors. Observe the phrases used by the best speakers.

Another similar complaint is that the missionary *does not understand the national*. This is particularly true of the missionary who continually uses conditions in the United States as a constant frame of reference. Also, the missionary may not be aware that he inadvertently at times goes against the customs of the people.

North Americans are noted for their frank approach. They are often in a hurry and want to get to the point without unnecessary preliminaries. Nationals in many areas prefer the oblique approach and avoid the direct statement, especially when it has to do with some form of accusation or judgment. They may not be so concerned with saving time as in not offending. An apparent assent may not really mean "yes," and if the missionary assumes that it does, he may find himself facing again the same problem when he thought that the matter had been settled. The missionary must become sensitive to the meaning behind oblique statements, and also he should attempt to moderate his own frankness and learn to convey thoughts and judgments in the same way that the nationals do.

Open discussion is essential to understanding. In this he must be careful not to monopolize conversation in order to get his point across. He should not do all the talking in committee meetings. Rather, he should encourage his fellow members to speak up. He must make room for the extra time required and not become frustrated with indirect approaches. By doing these things, perchance he may attain a degree of confidence and sharing with his brethren so that meaningful decisions can be reached to the satisfaction of all concerned.

Many times the North American missionary is thought to be *proud*. Sometimes this impression is communicated simply because the new missionary is not free in the language, and rather than make a mistake, he prefers to remain silent. His lack of communication could be mistaken for pride. It is better to make the effort to converse, even though mistakes are made in the language, than to give the impression of aloofness.

Although the missionary may be misunderstood at times, yet the *feeling of superiority* is something that the American missionary must constantly guard against. It can be manifested in so many different ways without the missionary even being aware of it. The missionary's education is often superior to that of those to whom he ministers. Then he probably enjoys a better financial position. This is manifested in his equipment and standard of living. This superiority may be manifested in the comparisons which the missionary makes between the customs of the people where he is working and the customs of his own home-land. His attitude toward his possessions is important. The spirit of sharing in God's work will help reduce tensions.

When a missionary bypasses the authority of the national church executives, he will certainly be considered as manifesting superiority. Such action shows the national that the missionary considers himself to be above the authority of the church.

There is sometimes the question as to whether the missionary *really loves* the people to whom he is ministering. Again, the missionary is open to misunderstanding in the area of financial help to the churches and to the pastors. He may desire wholeheartedly to develop initiative and responsibility in pastors and churches and thus refrain from making them dependent upon his financial help. This can very well be misinterpreted by some as lack of concern and love. Without sacrificing his ideal, the missionary must find ways to manifest his love other than by financial help.

Then there is the question of hospitality. Some missionaries do not invite nationals into missionary homes on the basis of friendship. This again is interpreted as stemming from a feeling of superiority and of lack of real friendship for the people.

To counterbalance these things, the missionary must attempt to develop sincere friendships and show interest in the national people. He can demonstrate that there is real love and concern in his heart by the way that he acts. Happily, nationals are usually highly intuitive in most cases and are able to discern a person's real thoughts and intent. It is not necessary for the missionary to make a statement to the effect that he loves them. His true feelings will show through and will win a response.

Of course, the matter is not one-sided. The missionary also may see things in the nationals that he does not approve of or which he may not understand. The missionary should be careful in making general statements. He should avoid categorizing the people as a group. For example: "These people are all liars"; "These people cannot be trusted." There are untrustworthy people in every society, including the missionary's homeland. All people are not alike. Such generalizations reflect a lack of penetration on the part of the speaker in the knowledge of the people and their culture.

However, the missionary may find that some nationals do not measure up to his standards in their responsibility in handling of funds. Some Christian concepts are attained only with Christian maturity. Patience is required. They also may seem to handle the truth loosely. This often must be interpreted in a cultural context. What might be a "lie" to a missionary may not be a lie to a national because both the one speaking and the person hearing understand what is really meant. True, nationals may not keep appointments on time and may be as much as an hour late to important meetings. These concepts are often culturally oriented, and it is the missionary who must make the adjustment. A Colombian asks, "Why should North Americans require strict punctuality in countries where the people keep their appointments by thinking in terms of hours rather than minutes? Why demand that work be delivered on time when the term *mañana* really only gives a certain degree of hope that the work will be eventually finished?"[2]

The missionary should avoid categorizing anyone as "stupid." This is a very offensive word and reveals more about the person who uses the term than it does about the person of whom it is spoken.

Some missionaries have developed tensions with the nationals because they have assumed that the nationals are looking for financial advantage and that the missionary or his equipment is just something that the national wants to "use." It will help the missionary to endeavor to see these things from the national's viewpoint. The missionary seems to have so much in comparison to the national. It is difficult for them to be objective. Some nationals, like their North American counterparts, are grasping and cannot be trusted. Care must be taken not to fall victim to their wiles, for this will mark the missionary as an "easy touch." However, again, we must not generalize and place all in the same category. Some are as sincere and generous as the missionary himself and are fully trustworthy. It is an injustice to look upon all with suspicion.

The fact that nationals do not always carry a project to conclusion or seem to lack initiative in these matters may also be annoying to the missionary. The missionary might examine the project under consideration to see if the project has really been accepted as the national's own. The lack of enthusiasm may stem from the fact that he never really was convinced of its necessity.

The lack of sanitation may become a tension-producing factor in the missionary's relationships with the nationals. Reasonable care must be taken to protect one's personal health and that of the family. However, some missionaries have become so germ-conscious in their concern about water, food, and personal contacts that a psychological barrier is raised between them and the nationals. Reasonable care for health is advisable, but love should so fill the heart that the concern is not primarily for one's own safety but rather to find the way of ministering to need. After all, the missionary goes to the foreign field not to save his life, but to lose it; not to minister to himself, but to others.

Slowness of individual response and lack of initiative can also be irritating to the missionary. This problem is usually culturally oriented, and if the missionary becomes aware of the reasons, it will help him to be more patient. For example, sometimes the missionary deals with people who have been accustomed all their life to taking orders from others. They have worked on plantations or haciendas. They carry over a certain passivity into their life in the church. It will take careful guidance and time for such an individual to understand that as God's child, filled with the Spirit, he, too, can make a contribution to the church.

Again, in some cultures, the individual is not expected to act on his own. He has always understood that important decisions are made by the family or the clan, and he does not feel comfortable when he is asked to make an individual decision without consulting with others.

In all of this the missionary should remember that he is called of God to minister to this people and that God will help him over the hurdles. There will be problems and difficulties to be ironed out. Hopefully, the missionary will learn to look at things through the national's eyes. While he is in the process of learning these things, he does have recourse to the love of God, which the Holy Spirit will shed abroad in his heart. Love is the bond of perfectness and the language of the heart. Tensions will be reduced and causes for difficulty minimized when love is truly manifest in our lives.

### Organizationally Oriented Tensions

The missionary's attitudes may be involved in a tension-producing situation. It could be that he may unconsciously suffer from a feeling of rejection. Possibly he has carried over from a previous period of ministry certain concepts concerning his ministry and his place in the national work that, while valid at one time, no longer pertain in the new situation. The initiative of the nationals in leadership may be interpreted as "anti-missionary," especially if the missionaries are not consulted in the decisions reached. This feeling of rejection may cause the missionary to resent the action and decisions of the national executives and consequently produce tensions in their relationships. Of course, the answer is for the missionary to take a square look at his own motives and at his goals in missionary work.

Along with this a missionary may attach too much importance to executive posts. Having been superintendent or having filled some other important position in the work, he now feels that he must take a secondary role and that actually his ministry is less important than it was before. It will help us to remember that the missionary's ministry is not primarily one of administrative responsibility and that the larger percent of administration has to do with maintaining the work and keeping the wheels of the organization running smoothly.

The primary ministry of a missionary is that of pioneer and church planter. Therefore, a missionary tied down with executive responsibilities, which perhaps builds the ego, may actually prove to be less fruitful in the area of ministry. Rather than a missionary resenting the fact that he is no longer filling executive posts, he should rejoice that he is now given the opportunity of fulfilling his more basic calling of planting and maturing the church.

Another cause of tensions and frustrations in this area is the fact that nationals are often immature and perhaps not as capable as the missionaries themselves. This is to be expected. We all learn by doing, and the national is no exception. It is also true that often the man who is the most desirous of executive posts is the least prepared spiritually for this responsibility. There is no question that some nationals are wrongly motivated in seeking nationals rather than missionaries to occupy executive posts. While some have the proper attitude and believe that the work would progress better under national leadership, others may be inspired by the motivation of personal ambition, and this can only produce friction and some measure of failure.

The missionary is called upon to exercise spiritual maturity in these circumstances. His faith in the Holy Spirit's ability to bring the church through victoriously needs to be coupled with patience and tact. Every missionary at such a time feels the need for divine wisdom and guidance. Perhaps the national church will make a mistake and put the wrong man into office. Let the missionary be slow to judge this and give his full cooperation, even if the man elected is not his own choice. Both the missionary and the church may learn valuable and necessary lessons through this experience. Missionaries sometimes have their own areas of carnality, and these circumstances are ideal means of showing them up! Given time the rough areas are likely to smooth out and understanding and happy relationships become the norm.

## The Goal of Harmonious Relationships

In a chapter called "Polarization and Harmony," which the author contributed to the book *Church/Missions Tensions Today*, there is outlined briefly the path that Assemblies of God missionaries have ordinarily taken to obtain a goal of national-missionary equality.

In order to attain this goal, a national organization has been formed early in the history of the work in each country, with a constitution which places the missionary and the national pastor on the same level of privilege. Election to official positions is limited only by the ability of each worker to meet the requirements of the constitution and to secure the backing of fellow workers. In several cases, national organizations have begun with as few as four or five churches. Quite logically, the missionaries fill posts of leadership in the beginning, since they have brought the work into existence, and the younger workers who are pastoring prefer that a missionary take this responsibility. In this position, the missionary teaches by example in the same manner that he has led the way in the development of other areas of church life. It is specifically desired that nationals fill all posts for which they are eligible. Often in the beginning, certain limitations of the constitution, requiring a stipulated degree of experience in the ministry for certain offices, are temporarily suspended to allow new workers to participate. This helps avoid a missionary-dominated organization. Admittedly, this procedure is somewhat risky, but we have not been disappointed in the outcome.

Usually our missionaries, attuned to the political climate of the country and being aware of the advantage of national brethren making their own decisions, seek to be relieved of their administrative posts as soon as possible. In a few cases they have insisted on this even before it seemed that the national ministers were actually ready for the change.

Since there are no restrictions on nationals filling executive positions, as soon as they have obtained sufficient maturity and experience to command the respect of their own brethren, there is a minimum of feeling that the missionary is smothering national initiative. This greatly mitigates against a power struggle between missionaries and nationals. In most cases, the transition to complete national leadership has been achieved without serious tensions.

However, since people are still people, some risks are involved. Usually before national leadership is attained with a corresponding partnership participation on the part of the missionaries, a certain oscillation between extreme positions is experienced. The progress has been more or less as follows:

1. The work is originally developed by missionaries prominent in leadership.

2. A national leadership develops in this situation, and usually if relationships between missionaries and national pastors have been wholesome and cordial, the first national superintendent will be someone close to the missionaries who has worked with them.

3. Often if the national superintendent is too much of a follower and depends too much on the missionaries, some dissatisfaction is likely to develop against him on the part of the more aggressive national leaders. They may complain that although the missionary is not superintendent, he is actually running the field through the superintendent, who is more or less a puppet.

4. The reaction against the national superintendent in this case may develop to the point that someone with more radical tendencies is placed in the office. At this stage, some of the nationals may be a little overconfident and the missionaries may feel that their ministry in the country is threatened. They may even feel unwanted. This is where maturity, understanding, and patience on the part of the missionary must be exercised.

5. At this juncture, one of two developments may transpire:

   a. The strong nationalistic leader may push his point of view too far, and a reaction against his policies may be the result. Being young and without too much experience, he may push his point of view so far that the more conservative element begins to assert itself again. The leader may find himself without sufficient following, and the post may go to someone else: either a missionary may be returned temporarily to the office or a more moderate national leader, who can avoid polarizing his position, will be placed in control. This latter creates a position whereby missionaries can work out a partnership relationship with the national church and enjoy fruit and growth for a long period.

b. The nationalistic leader may quickly learn that the work is more difficult than he had anticipated and modify his extreme position. If he comes to the conclusion that the missionary is not a threat to his position of leadership, a better understanding may be reached and he may come to the missionary for counsel and guidance in difficult questions.

Happily, many of the fields have avoided the problems of extremism, so the transition to complete national leadership has taken place in a tension-free atmosphere. So much depends upon the personalities involved; the greater the maturity and leadership among both nationals and missionaries, the smoother the transition will be.[3]

## Partnership Structures

Good relationships do not simply happen. They must be prayed about, planned for, and worked at patiently and consistently.

It will help to have some kind of structured relationship. There should be some channel through which the missionaries can approach the national executives and through which national executives can approach the missionaries in regard to problems or plans. Several of the national churches of their own accord have made room on their national executive committee for a missionary representative. He may be there with or without a vote, but he is there to monitor the attitudes of the national brethren and take note of the decisions made and convey these to the missionary body. Also, he represents the missionary body to the executive brethren for any project or problem that they may desire to present. This has proved very helpful.

Another device which we have found very helpful in ironing out missionary relations with the national executives is to call joint sessions in which all the leaders of the national church in all departments are present along with the entire missionary staff and in which they can talk over together the areas of relationships, problems, projects, and plans for the future, giving liberty for everyone to express his opinion. This provides an opportunity to work out tensions that may have developed and to also help the missionary find those areas of ministry where he can best serve the work. Such meetings should be planned at least once a year.

Whatever the structure, it is of utmost importance to have some medium of communication. Otherwise frustrations and tensions develop on both sides.

The writer recalls several occasions when he found it advisable as field secretary to call a joint meeting of national executives and missionaries. In these cases the national executive body was made up completely of national leaders, and missionaries had not a place in the administration of the work. In a couple of instances a missionary did sit as missionary representative in the national executive committee meetings. However, tensions developed, as missionaries in general felt "out of it." They were not aware of the thinking of the national brethren, and in turn, the national brethren were not well informed of the plans and activities of the missionaries. This gave room for suspicions and misunderstandings. We suggested a united conference in which both sides could air their complaints and ask questions. In every case it resulted in clearing the atmosphere and the bettering of relationships. Sometimes there were legitimate complaints and the causes needed to be corrected. Other times the matter was cleared up with explanations of what had actually happened. It was after observing the results of unity which such meetings produced that the writer urged that missionaries and national executives meet together at least once a year in planning sessions, in order to keep relationships on the highest possible level of understanding.

## *The Missionary Field Fellowship*

Up to this point, we have been more concerned about the individual missionary and his relationship to the national church. However, the missionary does not deal with the national church simply as an individual, but as one of a group of missionaries that has entered into a partnership with the national church in carrying out the Great Commission. There are advantages in having this relationship structured for the best possible relationships among the missionaries and to the national church.

One mission approaches the matter of missionary/national relations as follows:

> The major objective of the Missionary Field
> Fellowship shall be the establishing of an indigenous
> church. As soon as possible, a national organiza-
> tion shall be brought into being. After its establish-
> ment, all matters pertaining to the Church should be
> delegated to this national organization. The Field
> Fellowship should then concern itself exclusively
> with matters relating to the personal life of the mis-
> sionary in contrast to his ministry in and on behalf of
> the national church (*The Missionary Manual of the
> Assemblies of God*).

It is to be noted that there are limitations placed on the field fellowship in an effort to assure that the missionaries do not usurp the
prerogatives of the national organization nor vote in the national con-
ventions as a block. When either of these situations occur, they produce
tensions and are frustrating to the national leadership.

However, such restrictions should not be interpreted to mean that
the field fellowship is so separate from the national church that it
cannot so much as discuss the matters that concern it. This would be
unrealistic, for missionaries are on the field to work with the national
church, and it is important that missionaries discuss the problems and
programs so that they reach an understanding and consensus among
themselves.

For example, we have already explained that the place where a
missionary is to be stationed should be worked out with the national
church, and with the representatives of the mission, taking into account
the missionary's own calling and sense of divine direction. To give a
recommendation on this point certainly affects the national church. In
fact, the strategic placing of missionaries with a proper assignment
is one of the greatest contributions the mission can make toward the
development of the national church.

Other things also come into focus, such as whether a given project
merits a loan of missions funds. Again, what area of the country needs
development, and what can the mission do to stimulate the needed

growth? These are questions that affect the national church and must be discussed by the field fellowship. Also, the missionaries should come to some united understanding as to how funds will be handled, and if gifts are to be given to the national church, how they will be channeled. The restriction mentioned above is intended to insure that decisions belonging to the national church, such as issuing credentials to a worker or placing a pastor, shall not be usurped by the missionary.

It is important that the field fellowship operate in a way that will produce harmony among the missionaries themselves and understanding and cooperation with the national church. Great care must be taken, however, to insure that these deliberations of the missionary body do not in any way invade the prerogatives of the national church, but simply form the basis for discussion and interchange with the national officials or in the national assembly. The missionary should maintain an awareness of the influence of his words and position, not use these advantages in a way that will stifle the proper initiative in decision making on the part of the national church itself.

Of course, it is necessary that both the missionaries and the national executives approach the area of relationships with proper attitudes. The missionary must accept the national executives in their role and not carry over relationships based on the past when the man who is now a national leader was once just a student in school or a young preacher. Some missionaries have taken the attitude, "Well, he may be the national superintendent, but I remember the little town where he came from, and for me he will always be just 'Little John.'"

Missionaries must honor agreements that are reached in the national church even when they have not originated with them. If the missionary is a member of the national organization, he probably will have the same responsibilities, financial and otherwise, that fall upon the national workers, and these should be honored, although there may be special cases where some adjustment would have to be made because of financial obligations elsewhere.

Also, the missionary should not bypass the national executive. It is extremely frustrating to the national officer who is purportedly in charge of a certain section of the work to have the missionary disregard him and handle a problem unilaterally, as though there were no superintendent, secretary, or presbyter involved.

Spiritual maturity is the key. There has never been a time in the history of missions when the missionary enterprise needed men of mature spiritual character, with the fruit of the Spirit, more than today. Naturally, we would expect also that the national executives would show spiritual maturity, but here is where the missionary can show the way. If others are small or ambitious and fail to manifest the right attitude, let the missionary give the example of what true Christian leadership is. There are no restrictions to abounding in love!

## *Endnotes*

[1] Wagner, C. Peter, *Latin American Theology* (Grand Rapids, Mich.: Eerdmans) 1970.

[2] Márquez, Jairo, *Anatomía del Gringo* (Bogotá, Colombia: Ediciones Tercer Mundo) 1966.

[3] Wagner.

# 5

# Missionary Relationships

## *The Missionary Field Structure*

The term *field fellowship* or *missionary field council* refers to the approved structure for the coordinated effort among missionaries on a given field in foreign lands. It will soon become apparent to the new missionary that work on the mission field is different than in the homeland. Most new missionaries have come from a background of a pastorate. The question of close cooperation with his fellow ministers was not too important. He could do his work in his own church and let the other man carry out his own program in his church.

The problem is complicated on the mission field because, at least to a measure, we work with the same people. What one missionary does affects every other missionary on the field. For example, if one missionary feels as a matter of principle that he should be conservative in the matter of handing out funds to nationals, and he considers this important in the building of the national church, he will be dismayed and feel frustrated if his fellow missionaries do not share these same ideals and hand out money freely. Not only so, but it will not be too long before the nationals begin to make comparison of one missionary with another and measure their appreciation for the missionary by the amount of money he distributes. Thus, one man's generosity makes another man appear stingy and unloving.

## The Individual and the Team

In a team effort, who makes the point is not as important as the winning of the game. Every player must subject his own personal will and desires to the good of the game. First Corinthians 12 gives us an even higher concept of cooperation. There we are compared to members of a body working together under one Head.

Probably every individual missionary has a primary concern for the success of his own ministry. This is really, however, only a part of the picture. Three things must be brought into line for a satisfactory team effort on the mission field. The missionary must work with his fellow missionaries, and the missionaries as a group must work with the church and with the national organization that governs that church. Finally, the missionary's own particular call and ministry must be satisfied.

The missionary's own personal abilities and ministries and the situation of his family should be taken into account. Health problems must sometimes be considered in regard to the location of a missionary. While it perhaps should not be the determining factor, schooling for the missionaries' children also becomes an important factor in the location of a missionary family. All of these considerations contribute to making missionary work a most complex activity today. Missionaries must strive to remember that they are not simply individuals, but are members of a body.

Rivalry should be unknown in the work of God. However, missionaries, like God's people everywhere, have not yet attained their true stature in Christ. Consequently, rivalries and selfishness are manifested among missionaries. Some seem to want to build a kingdom for themselves instead of building the kingdom of God. Perhaps this is unconscious in many cases. We can hide selfishness behind our zeal for the Lord.

Someone has pointed out that the ministry affords an ideal situation for developing selfishness. It sometimes takes the form of ambition for office, sometimes that of having a more shining report for the folks at home. We have seen missionaries become upset because their supporting churches were contacted by the mission office for help on a project in their country, but which did not particularly benefit their own area. The question of which missionary has the better housing or furniture can evoke envy on the part of some.

How important it is for missionaries to remember that they are not rivals but partners in the work of the Lord: We are a body, and if one member prospers, we should rejoice with him rather than being envious of the harvest that he was able to reap. As members of the same body, no one can rob us of our place if we exercise faith, humility, and obedience to God. How often has the work of God been hindered because His servants did not hold these truths in proper perspective.

## The Individual and Body Ministry

We now come to the difficult problem of harmonizing individual initiative with the concept of body ministry. Some persons, in a reaction to ecclesiastical machinery and bondage, have insisted they take their orders individually from the Head of the Church. It is probable that too many of us think of our ministry in terms of a modern Samson or Elijah. We tend to forget we are living in a new era and that the highest norm of ministry in the New Testament is body ministry. This is emphasized over and over again in the teaching of the epistles.

A good example of the solution to this problem can be found in the life of Paul himself. He received his call at the time of his conversion (Acts 9). In Galatians 2 we are told that he conferred not with flesh and blood but went to Arabia and received the revelation of the gospel he preached. He goes so far as to say that Peter and John, pillars in the church, added nothing to him.

However, in the actual carrying out of his ministry, we see him waiting for God's time and for the approval of the church. This came when the Holy Spirit said, "Set apart for me Barnabas and Saul for the work to which I have called them" (Acts 13:2). They were already called, but they needed the confirmation and the backing of the church. Note, too, that Paul states he was commanded by God to go up to Jerusalem (Galatians 2:1,2), and lay before the brethren the doctrine he preached among the Gentiles "for fear that [he] was running or had run [his] race in vain." Paul without doubt knew his revelation was from

God yet realized that he must also submit to his brethren. Otherwise, there might have been two Christian churches in the beginning: the Pauline church and the Jerusalem church. Paul could afford to submit his divine revelation for the approval of his brethren. He trusted the Holy Spirit to illuminate them. We are on safe ground in seeking that the church endorse our individual guidance and ministry.

## *The Organization of a Field Fellowship*

It is logical for missionaries sent out by the same board to the same area to organize some kind of a field fellowship or field council. Otherwise, every missionary will be left to his own devices and there will be no coordination of evangelism or other projects.

In reading the account of Paul's missionary journey in the Book of Acts, it becomes apparent that at first Barnabas was the leader, and later Paul became the head of the missionary band that accompanied him, and he coordinated the activities of the team. The members did not operate independently of one another. When John Mark returned home without the approval of the leaders, he was subject to censure (Acts 12:25; 13:5,13; 15:37–39).

In much the same way, each missionary coming to the field with the approval of the home office must understand that he must cooperate with field leadership and form a part of the team. He is not to take his own initiative in promoting projects and raising money for them among his supporting churches, or appoint workers on his own to follow up his campaigns. Such matters affect other missionaries, and if there is a national organization, it is also involved. The field fellowship should be organized with its own chairman and officers and have a simple constitution to guide it in its operation. Decisions should be reached in a proper manner with all members having the opportunity of expressing their opinion.

Every missionary granted appointment automatically becomes a member of the field fellowship. In a well-organized missionary effort there is no such thing as a missionary appointed to a field who is not also a member of the field fellowship. The missionary program cannot be run by remote control. For the home office to handle each problem separately without reference to field leadership would only bring confusion.

The field fellowship is the structure through which the missionary effort can be coordinated with the national church and with the missionary team. It is important then that the missionary understand his relationship to the field fellowship and to the national work. It is understood that decisions made by the field fellowship are subject to review by the home board.

Businesslike procedures should be followed in the session of the missionary field fellowship. When business is to be taken up, an agenda should be made with each missionary having the opportunity of putting items on the agenda that he believes should be discussed. Then the chairman should bring up the items on the agenda one by one, leaving ample room for discussion. The decision should be reached by a motion, a vote should be taken, and the decision recorded in the minutes.

During the time the field fellowship is not in session, certain responsibilities will be placed in the hands of the executive field fellowship committee. These officers are to take care of business for the field fellowship under the guidelines that the field fellowship has set forth. Such decisions made must be reported back to the field fellowship in the next meeting. Financial reports are given so that the members of the field fellowship know how the finances have been handled.

The field fellowship has responsibilities to the World Missions Board and to the national church. The officers of the field fellowship should be chosen on the basis of mature judgment and capabilities. It should not be a matter simply of personal preference. The chairmanship should not be shifted from one missionary to another every year. Missionary leadership on the field should have an opportunity to develop. The field fellowship needs to engage in long-range planning. This cannot be done when there is a constant shift of executive personnel.

## The Importance of Attitudes

As members of a field fellowship, personal attitudes are important. Individual missionaries must keep in mind the total objectives of the field. A missionary's interests should go beyond his own individual activity and sphere. There should also be concern for the success of fellow missionaries. We should do our best to help them to succeed. This is particularly true in the relationship of older missionaries to younger missionaries. The field chairman and the committee have a responsibility to young missionaries.

The sending board also should become involved in insuring the success of new missionaries and do everything possible to help them overcome the obstacles they may face. Some have found that it is helpful to set up an evaluation program for new missionaries during their probationary term as first-termers. The purpose of the evaluation is not judgmental but corrective, with the idea of giving the new missionary a chance to correct mistakes before he comes to the end of his term. If older missionaries will take the Christlike attitude that Barnabas took with Paul in order to help him get started in his ministry, they will be doing a service to the body of Christ (Acts 9:26–28; 11:25,26).

On the other side of the coin, new missionaries should not be quick to discount the labor and effort that have gone into the work up to that point. It is a common failure of all of us to see weaknesses rather than strong points. There have been first-term missionaries with less than a year's experience on the field who have roundly criticized the older missionaries, stating that things were not being done correctly. Actually they should have been listening and learning rather than passing judgments. Perhaps the young missionary may be correct in his assessments, but the probabilities are that given a little more time and more insight into the problems faced on the field, the criticism would be less caustic and more sympathetic and constructive. Younger missionaries should show appreciation for the effort of those who have gone before them. Someone has said, "Youth is like a child born in the night who sees the sunrise and thinks that there never was a yesterday."

Missionaries, whether junior or senior, should learn to trust one another. Give the benefit of the doubt to the other person. We must try to put ourselves in the other person's shoes and remember that people do not have to be perfect in order to have our love. Let us make room for each other in our hearts. When we help each other, we help ourselves, and we help the body of Christ.

The field fellowship should not be just a time of business, dealing with the problems that confront the missionary family, but it should also be a time of warm spiritual fellowship. Let not the area of prayer fellowship be neglected in the meetings. Rather, let missionaries pray for one another, love one another, and help one another. It has proved profitable to set aside a full day for spiritual fellowship, encouragement, and prayer in the yearly meeting before the items of business are taken up.

# 6

# The Overseas Church and Missionary Finance

The matter of church finance is closely related to the previous chapter on the missionary's partnership with the national church. The case for a church which supports its own ministry and depends upon its own financial resources has been presented in detail in the author's books.[1] Here we will merely summarize the dangers of depending on foreign funds and the benefits of self-support for the purpose of providing a proper background for decisions that must be made in the present situation.

## Importance of Self-Support

The danger of depending on foreign support for salaries of pastors and the maintenance of the work may be itemized as follows:

*There is a danger to the church itself.* Sometimes instead of helping, subsidy often destroys the very principle that will produce a strong vital church. It has been amply demonstrated that for a church to depend upon foreign sources for its finances kills its initiative and deadens the sense of responsibility.

We might draw a comparison from those wild animals that have been found in time of infancy by nature-loving people and raised in the shelter of their home. The animal is deprived of the hardships of the struggle for existence, and if it must revert to its natural state, it may perish either from lack of sufficient food or because it has not learned to defend itself against its natural enemies. Or like the sea gulls of the Gulf Coast that learned to depend upon the shrimp boats to provide them food from the refuse of the catch; they finally became so dependent upon the fishing fleet that when it was removed the gulls did not know how to fend for themselves and perished. An old proverb says, "Give a man a fish, and you help him for a day; teach him to fish, and you help him for the rest of his life."

One has only to look at the strong, indigenous, evangelical churches in certain sections of the world to see a demonstration of the fact that churches do better when they learn to depend upon their own resources. In some cities missions are struggling with small congregations with mission-paid pastors, and the congregations have had their churches built for them with foreign funds. In those same cities, large congregations in the midst of the same poverty, usually without foreign help from abroad, have built large church buildings and are carrying on a vital and rapidly expanding evangelistic program. Surely this should say something to us.

*The second danger is to the worker himself.* We develop when our faith is put to the test. Struggle and sacrifice have their part in the development of every man of God. God has His own way of maturing workers, which is often thwarted when we supply artificial help from foreign funds. The worker learns to depend upon the mission instead of upon God. This is also a cause of deep conflicts between missionaries and national workers, since rarely does the mission have enough funds at its disposal to actually pay the worker an adequate salary. Tensions that are produced result in anti-missionary feeling.

This brings us to another vital point. If the church in a given country is dependent upon mission funds, it goes without saying that *the work cannot advance any further than the supply line will permit.* The limit to expansion is imposed by the limitation of funds. This is an impossible situation for the Church of Jesus Christ. In this day when the nations of the world are demanding to exercise complete freedom from foreign domination, it is an anachronism for the church to be placed in a situation where the possibility of its advance is dictated by the amount of foreign funds available.

Also the subsidizing of a church by a foreign mission *projects the public image of a foreign-dominated work.* If the church is to grow, it must be seen as something that, by its inherent nature, can grow in any culture. Foreign missions support will project the opposite image. The church is seen in such cases as the introduction of a foreign religion, and often related to imperial domination. No matter how earnestly and honestly the mission may desire that the church expand in its own right, the fact that the money for the support of the church comes from the foreign mission carries with it the idea of control. The nationals realize that the mission could cut off its support at any time. The church does not have true freedom to make its own decisions when its very existence depends on foreign funds.

A somewhat subtle argument for foreign support of overseas churches has been brought forward and emphasized recently. The Church is one, it is said, and the Church in different areas has different needs. If one country needs personnel, then perhaps a teacher or an evangelist could be sent. The church that has such individuals should share them with the church that does not have them. In some countries the church has personnel but does not have the finances to support them. The church that has the finances should supply funds to the church that is lacking them. We cannot accept this argument without qualifications. To do so would be to overlook other important factors.

It is true that the Church is one, and what is lacking in one area may be supplied from another part of the Body. However, we do violence to the concept of the responsibility of the members of the body of Christ if we interpret this to mean that certain members are thereby excused from doing what they rightfully should do. For example, the fact that one church in one country may have a good evangelist and can supply an evangelistic ministry to another church does not relieve the receiving church from evangelizing. It must still carry its own responsibility in soul-winning. Likewise, the fact that one church may have more financial resources than another church does not mean that the poorer church is relieved of its responsibility of paying tithes and supporting its own minister. The generosity of one church should not be an excuse for another church to fail to fulfill its responsibilities. Louis King at the Green Lake Missions Executive Conference said, "No church can successfully assume another church's obligation to biblical faith, life and mission."[2]

The benefits to a church that finds its own resources for its maintenance and expansion are thus evident. The church is likely to be more vital, more alive, and more responsible. Further, there is no limit to the amount of expansion that can be experienced. The minister can enjoy the freedom of exercising faith in God for his support rather than depending on a mission.

## A Sense of Responsibility

All of this does not mean that there is never a time that foreign funds should be used to stimulate or help the work of God overseas. There are times and places where outside money can be helpful. The missionaries' task is to determine when financial aid will strengthen or weaken the church. *A sense of responsibility* is a "pearl of great price" in the overseas church and its ministry. The overseas church must be a church in its own right, never a second-class church that cannot govern itself, support itself, or develop its own ministries. Anything that a missionary does to help this church to realize its true mission is in order. Everything he does that diminishes this sense of responsibility and makes the church more dependent upon him or his organization is a sin against the church. So, if he will ask himself the question, "Will this gift make this church more dependent on me or the mission, or will it help the church to realize its own identity under God and function as a true church?" then this will serve as a criterion to determine where and how help should be given. A word of warning: let us not reach the conclusion too quickly that the church is unable to assume financial responsibility. The church when thrown back on its own resources will often do that which missionaries thought could not be done.

Basically, mission help should be given to help the church attain its goals. Mission help should never be a *substitute* for self-help. The mission should not do for a church what it is unwilling to do for itself. This is why self-support and self-government are so closely aligned. The process of decision making is important to the assuming of responsibility.

Further, the missionary must distinguish between short-term and long-term benefits. It is entirely possible that a gift of money may prove to be of temporary benefit but may in the long run tend to make the church dependent. For example, the construction of a church building with foreign funds may result in immediate growth and increase, but at the cost of engendering expectations on the part of other congregations that their building will also be provided for them. Why should they struggle and sacrifice if by patiently waiting the missionary will arrange to have it built for them?

It would seem to be in order for financial help to be given in the training program to prepare ministers for the fulfilling of their vocation. Also, it is logical to help provide a building as a base for a church in a large city where the cost of property is so high that it is completely beyond the reach of the local congregation. Even so, this help should be given in such a way that it will not become a "missions project." The local congregation should be expected to assume its responsibility and make the sacrifices to construct the building, understanding that the mission is giving them a boost to help them on their way, but is not doing the job for them.

## Church Properties

The question of how properties will be held becomes an important question. In these days when most countries have restrictions about foreign-held properties, it would seem to be the part of wisdom to turn as many church properties over to the national organization as possible. Probably Bible institute properties will be the last to be transferred to the national organization. However, there is no reason that this should not be done once the national organization has reached a state of maturity and experience in fiscal matters to insure proper handling. In some cases, because of local laws, the national organization has become the owner of these properties from the very beginning, and this has not usually resulted in problems.

Missions would do well to hold loosely to the material aspects of their missionary endeavor. Properties, like individuals, are expendable. It is the Church that must go on.

## Endnotes

[1] Hodges, Melvin L., *The Indigenous Church* (Springfield, Mo.: Gospel Publishing House, 1971); also published as *Growing Young Churches* (Chicago, Ill.,: Moody Press). Dr. Hodges also produced a companion book, *Build My Church,* addressed to national church leaders.

[2] Wagner, C. Peter, *Latin American Theology* (Grand Rapids, Mich.: Eerdmans) 1970.

# 7

# The Missionary
# and Evangelism

Evangelism is the very heart of the missionary ministry. Evangelism is what missionary work is all about. Of the three basic factors of the indigenous church, propagation of the gospel is the most important.

## The Goal of Evangelism

Evangelism needs a definition. Self-propagation as it relates to the Church is a little more definitive. When we speak of evangelism, we are not referring simply to handing out literature or preaching on a street corner, although these may be included in evangelistic activities. Evangelism includes, first, the proclamation of the gospel to the unconverted; second, the persuading of men to accept Christ and to come to a personal relationship with him; third, helping these converts to find their place as members of a local church. In the New Testament example and teaching, there seems to be no place for simply making converts without relating them to local churches. The work of evangelism is not terminated until converts have found their place as functioning members of the body of Christ.

In the pioneer stages of missionary work, the missionary's contribution to evangelism is self-evident. This is what he went to do: preach the gospel, win men to Christ, and form churches. Later when some churches have already been formed, and perhaps there is a national organization serving these churches, the question arises, "What can the missionary now do toward the main objective of evangelism?"

## Twofold Missionary Contribution

The missionary's contribution to evangelism falls naturally in two parts: first, that which he can do himself as an individual minister and Christian to win men to Christ; and second, what he can do by teaching and inspiring others, thus stimulating the churches to carry out their evangelistic ministry.

There is an all-too-common tendency for missionaries to become less and less involved personally in evangelism. When the missionary first goes to a field, evangelism is his primary responsibility; his efforts are expended mainly in traveling to new areas—the opening of preaching points and in personal witness and persuasion. As the years go by, he finds it constantly more difficult to engage in his primary ministry. Many things crowd in. There is the administrative work of the mission, the teaching in the Bible school, the special conferences—so that in the end he may find that very little of his time is given to presenting Christ to the unconverted. The missionary must continually make a conscious effort to correct this. We must not forget that we are called to reconcile men to God. Let every missionary strive constantly in prayer and seek the help of the Spirit to keep this vision and ministry alive.

## Avenues of Missionary Evangelism

There is, of course, a distinct possibility that a missionary may continue in his primary evangelistic ministry even after there are churches formed and a national organization is functioning. Actually, there is no reason for believing that a national organization is prepared immediately to assume the total responsibility of evangelism with all that this involves.

Usually, even though the national organization is formed, the churches exist in only certain sections of the country. There will be entire states or provinces without any church and perhaps others with only one or two. Now, this presents an opportunity for the continuance of missionary ministry. And happily enough, this is normally what the national church desires the missionary to do. In my experience, the anti-missionary feeling has developed particularly in those areas where missionaries are clustered in the capital or larger cities rather than getting out into the outlying areas and establishing churches.

There are, of course, many reasons why missionary families stay in capital cities. One is that they are often required to teach in the Bible institute. Another very important consideration is the education of the missionary children. Often the schooling available is not adequate in the outlying districts, and to go outside of the capital city means that the missionary must undertake to teach his own children or else send them away to a boarding school. Naturally, these are alternatives that many times are unacceptable to a missionary, and so he stays in the capital.

Many things determine the decision. When the country is small geographically, it may be that the capital provides ready access to every section of the country, and nothing would really be gained by moving out to a smaller town. At other times the family situation is such that the choice is either to stay in the capital or withdraw temporarily from missionary service in order to place the children in school. The general policy of some missions requires that parents send their children to boarding school when they reach a certain age so that the parents may be free to minister in the area of greatest need. This is often harder on the parents than on the children, and while there are exceptions, the sending of children away to boarding school has not had unfavorable consequences as a general rule. We do not attempt at this point to generalize or give directions to missionary families. We simply point out that often there are opportunities to go out into the provinces. When a family has preschool children, the parents are still free to live in more isolated surroundings. Also, the missionaries whose children have already left home could return again to this type of ministry. Others will find a way to give their children the needed schooling and move to an outlying department. What is important here is the motivation and the vision.

After fifteen years of missionary service, it is easy to allow secondary considerations to deprive us of our primary missionary ministry. In the beginning of a missionary ministry, we are often willing to make very real sacrifices to see the work progress. It does not necessarily follow, because we started this way, that this same level of consecration and dedication will continue. It requires the continual work of the Holy Spirit in our hearts to keep us alert and alive to the opportunities and challenges before us.

Another way a missionary may help in evangelism is through conducting campaigns in larger cities. This will, of course, depend upon whether he has an evangelistic ministry. He may do this himself as an evangelist, or he may simply be the man who inspires and arranges for the evangelistic campaigns.

National church leaders have a point when they say that the missionary has facilities for evangelistic and pioneer work that they do not have. Often he has a car and public address systems. Sometimes he either has a tent or could secure one. He may have funds available to rent an auditorium. Above all, he has mobility, which is something a national may lack and which may multiply his difficulties. In no sense is this an excuse for nationals not getting into active evangelistic work and pioneering new areas. However, if the national pastors see the missionary with all of his equipment and abilities staying in the city and seemingly indifferent to evangelism, it has an adverse effect upon a national's vision. Why should he make sacrifices that men of supposedly greater consecration, ability, and with more facilities fail to make?

Campaigns in the city do not necessarily require a building. A tent is very useful, and in the absence of this, an open lot in a dry season can be very productive. It does not cost too much to erect a temporary platform, string some lights up, connect public address systems, and invite the public to an open-air meeting. At least in Latin America, hundreds will come to an open-air meeting who would not think of going into a Protestant church. Dozens and perhaps hundreds of churches have been started in this manner.

## *Evangelism by Teaching*

The second part of the missionary's contribution in encouraging evangelism and self-propagation is in what he can do through others by teaching and guiding his national brethren.

One of the greater ministries open today to missionaries working with the national church is that of teaching among the churches. Many of the churches need to be inspired with vision for the evangelizing of their neighborhood. We all have seen comparatively small congregations of one or two hundred people happily content in a section of a large city of perhaps a half-million inhabitants, making no real effort to reach the city. They work with the relatives of the members, with the friends they bring to the services, or with the strangers that may drop in during a campaign, and they feel that they have done their duty. Perhaps ten blocks away, not one in five people know that the church exists.

To make matters worse, sometimes the pastor of the church will object to another effort being made in the city, feeling that he has a franchise on the whole city. This is a deplorable situation that needs to be corrected. Missionaries can make a valuable contribution to such churches by imparting to them the vision of winning a lost world for Christ. He can further show them methods by which the church can reach out. We have often emphasized that every church is responsible for all the territory around, at least halfway to the next church.

Recently, in a medium-sized city, one of the pastors came to a missionary[1] who was emphasizing the ministry of the lay members and said to him, "What can I do? I have about sixty members, and I have been preaching to them for about two years. We seldom see an outsider in the church, and very few people are converted in our services. We have services every night of the week. There are Bible studies and young peoples' meetings, women's meetings," etc. The missionary replied, "Close down your services for two weeks, except on Sundays. Get your members to invite you to a different home every night of the week. Have them invite their neighbors and friends to a house meeting. Then go from place to place during the week. Invite them all to come in to church on Sunday." After two weeks the national pastor reported to the missionary, "Can you believe it? I have preached to sixty-eight new people in these two weeks, more new people than I have preached to in the church in two years."

Branch Sunday Schools provide another way to reach out into the community. In one Central American city, one church with about eighty members trained twenty-five Sunday School workers and at one given time reached two thousand people over one weekend. Sunday School classes were held in homes of believers and even in the homes of the unconverted. Some classes were held in a park under trees.

Every Christian is a witness for Jesus Christ. God expects every converted person to tell what he has found in Jesus. To witness is a natural result of having met Christ. When the love of God fills a person's heart, he wants to tell others about it. There is usually an absence of inhibitions in the newly converted Christian. He wants to share. The problem is that the newly converted Christian often sees older Christians who seemingly are unconcerned or indifferent about spreading the gospel. He learns from them, quenches the Spirit, and finally becomes just another church member sitting in the pew, not really involved in God's work. Often the missionary can show a better way, and the church can establish a different pattern.

We have elsewhere explained how a church can fill the area with preaching points, using lay members to carry on this work. Some of these preaching points should develop into churches that will continue to spread the gospel and establish other preaching points and churches. Actually, it is better to have twenty smaller churches with one hundred members each, scattered throughout the city, than to have one great church with two thousand members. Both are important, and we do not underrate the big church with its appeal and ministry to a class of people that the small church will not reach. But, block by block and individual by individual, several smaller churches are more likely to do the job of total evangelism in a city. Happily, there is a place for both large and small churches.

Every church should consider itself a mother church and seek to establish daughter churches throughout the area. It is a tragedy when the vision of the church becomes inverted so that the members think only of their own needs and of maintaining their own program. Some pastors are quite content to carry on with the church as long as the offerings are sufficient to pay their salary. They feel that in maintaining the church, they are discharging their duty. The missionary may help to inspire pastors and churches with the vision of total evangelism.

## Lay Workers' Training

Another area of need in the carrying out of this evangelistic outreach is the training of the lay workers who will be going to take care of the preaching points. The pastor of each church may give some training, but the pastor himself often needs help to know how to teach these budding workers. The missionary would do well to prepare courses that the pastors may teach to their own workers. This would include the subjects such as "How to Direct a Service," "The Standards of Christian Living," "Prayer," and "House-to-House Evangelism." In fact, the missionary himself can move among the churches with courses of this nature. If the situation permits, several churches could come together for a couple of weeks of study. Perhaps there is no greater contribution a missionary can make than this teaching ministry to local churches. This effort is further explained in the following chapter under the heading "Teaching for Christian Maturity" (page 196).

The missionary who is called upon to teach in a Bible school can have a powerful influence on the students by presenting the vision and methods for evangelism. He must, however, have a heart filled with evangelistic fervor. It is not enough to present the material in a methodical manner simply with the objective that the students get a good grade on their examinations. The teacher must have the fire of evangelism in his soul. He should also lead the way by example. The Bible school is vital in the development of the national church, since the students who go through the school will normally be the leaders of the church in the future. How important it is then that the Bible school not simply be a place to learn theory, but where the students are inspired and led in this primary ministry of winning souls and establishing churches.

The time spent in Bible school should be a time not only for acquiring knowledge but also for practical work in evangelism. The students should not lose contact with the world around them. Weekends should be spent as much as possible in evangelistic activities.

## Evangelistic Centers

Beginning some twenty-five years ago there was a move toward establishing great evangelistic centers, especially in the large cities. Usually, it was thought of these in terms of being a center for large campaigns. A bookstore, a radio program, and perhaps a night school for Bible training was to be a part of the regular activities for the evangelistic center. It was not anticipated that this evangelistic center would develop into a church, but that it would become the center from which converts could go out and establish churches throughout the city. Experience has proved that in general, these evangelistic centers usually become large churches and operate as such.

There are some problems in regard to the concept of an evangelistic center. For one thing, if it is envisioned that a missionary will be in control with national helpers for an indefinite period of time, this inevitably produces some areas of tension within the national organization, for the center can easily become a sort of missionary island within the national organization.

How does the evangelistic center fit into the national organization? In order to give continuity to its ministry and meet the financial obligation, it is necessary to have regular membership. The center needs the financial support of the people. So the evangelistic center becomes their church home. Thus, at times a church has been brought into existence whose relationship with the rest of the churches is not too clear.

Another problem is the fact that people who go out from evangelistic centers as workers do not really have sufficient experience in the operation of a regular church unless the evangelistic center engages in a church planting ministry. They know how to run an evangelistic center, but not a church.

Probably one of the biggest problems has been the fact that the missionaries who have been in charge of the evangelistic centers have developed a different type of program than is carried on by the local churches. Many outside visitors such as renowned evangelists, in coming to the city, came to the evangelistic center and bypassed the little churches. This caused some resentment. Also, when the center held a big meeting, the other churches felt that it attracted the people away from their own churches.

Not the least of the problems lies in when and how to make an evangelistic center "indigenous." The difference between the level of a missionary's ministry and that of the national brother has sometimes been too great to bridge.

Some of the advantages of the evangelistic center are:

1. It is usually made to accommodate a much larger group of people and gives a sense of stability to the work.

2. The people of a better class in the community are likely to find themselves more at home in an evangelistic center with its larger congregation and an atmosphere more congenial to their culture.

3. When the center has remained faithful to its purpose, it has often been the means of starting other churches throughout the city.

So much depends on the leadership and clearly outlined long-range goals. It is evident that the plan to run the center without its being a church is not practical. The church formed in the center should submit to all the rules and regulations of the national organization. A clearly outlined constitution showing its relationship to the national organization will be helpful. Open communications are absolutely necessary.

One of the most successful operations of an evangelistic center that has come to the writer's attention is that of San Salvador, capital of El Salvador, Central America. It was established in a time of evangelistic outreach in the city, and there were about twelve other small churches of the same denomination in the city at the time of its founding. For one regular Sunday in May 1975, the Sunday School report on attendance read as follows:

| | |
|---|---|
| In the evangelistic center itself | 890 |
| In the center's outstations of the center | 2,877 |
| In the 8 annexes related to the center | 9,029 |
| TOTAL | 12,796 |

Certain factors contributed to the growth and stability of this evangelistic center:

1. It has a clear agreement with the national church body.
2. Its director is a Spanish-American missionary, raised by missionary parents in Latin America. His acceptance is that of a Latin American.
3. The church supports two co-pastors. The director is gradually withdrawing from the center to leave it more completely in the hands of the national ministers.
4. It sponsors a large day school with over a thousand students that covers the entire area from primary through high school, yet this school is largely self-supporting. The school provides a channel of contact with many families otherwise unreached by the gospel.
5. The director has fired the congregation with the challenge of discipleship and evangelism.
6. The outstation system, so fruitful in Central America, has been used by the center with profit with an addition.
7. The outstations stay for a longer period of time under the umbrella of the evangelistic center. The center provides them first with a rented house or hall, and one of the local lay preachers of the center becomes the pastor while still retaining his employment. The center endeavors to help each outstation (at this stage called an annex) to secure its own building. Then the annex can move toward autonomy, supporting its own pastor, and finally being set in order as an autonomous church of the national organization. One has been thus organized and others are in the process. It is felt that by not severing the ties with the mother church too quickly, it gives a certain security to the young church and a sense of belonging to a successful evangelical community.

## Encouraging Missions

Finally, missionaries should lead churches in a vision for missions beyond their country. Missionaries have gone to foreign fields because of the missionary vision others passed on to them. Certainly they have not waited until all the cities were evangelized in their homeland before they went out. Why then should they wait until the whole country is reached by the gospel before they present to them the challenge of carrying the gospel to the ends of the earth?

Admittedly, there are problems, one of the chief of which is lack of finances. Yet we know that churches in the U.S.A., which also have great needs themselves, take up regular missionary offerings to send the gospel abroad. Do we do well when we withhold this vision and challenge from the churches overseas?

Happily, in some areas of the world, the national church has already begun to send out missionaries—sometimes to neighboring tribes, sometimes to neighboring countries, and occasionally across the sea. Some national churches have already formed missions departments. This is to be encouraged. The missionary would do well to resurrect some of the missionary sermons he preached to the churches at home and preach them again to the younger churches overseas.

Let us pass to the national churches the torch of world evangelism we ourselves have received and the vision that impelled us to go to the regions beyond, so that every church and every individual may truly feel a part of the worldwide outreach of the universal Church.

## Endnote

[1] Reported by Arthur Lindvall, an Assemblies of God missionary to Latin America.

# 8

# Initiating Services for the National Church

As the national church develops, new and pressing needs call for attention. Opportunities present themselves that require all of the ingenuity and strength of missionaries and nationals alike to bring the almost unlimited possibilities to fruition. Some of the more pressing needs are:

1. Advanced education for national leaders and Bible institute teachers.
2. Maturation of the Christians in the national churches.
3. Literature for the unsaved, the Christian, the pastor, and text-books for Bible institutes.
4. Some plan and activity of evangelism that will inspire and mobilize the church to reach the unevangelized areas of the country.

In the period of the writer's administrative work in Latin America, programs to help meet these needs began to be developed. One of the first and important steps was the bringing together of national leadership in the various countries of Latin America for area conferences in which the needs of the work could be discussed with missionaries and nationals. Since Latin America extends over such a wide area, we finally broke these area conferences down into three sections: (1) the southern section of South America; (2) the northern section of South America with Central America; and (3) the West Indies. Such conferences were aided in Latin America by the fact that we had main languages in which to work. Spanish was the language of the bulk of the countries. The large country of Brazil spoke Portuguese. The West Indies were divided among English, Spanish, and French. However, the problem was complicated by the fact that many of these areas were in different stages of development. Hence, their needs were different.

## Program of Christian Education

About the time that area conferences were being initiated, an effort was made to evaluate our Bible institute work for the preparation of pastors. Several men and women prominent in Bible school work were brought together and spent six weeks evaluating the programs. Latin America had a wide divergence in Bible institute programs since these grew out of the initiative of the missionaries involved. Schools ran for different lengths of time, and different subjects were taught. Some were fairly sophisticated, and others were quite simple.

From this study, a basic plan for Bible schools evolved which was to become the basis of evaluation for Bible schools throughout Latin America. In our area conferences, special committees composed of national leaders and missionaries were formed for the purpose of encouraging Christian education in the different national churches. Finally, the new Bible school committees working in the Spanish area together with representatives from the Portuguese area met for intensive study of the Bible institute situation and approved the basic plan as a guide to all of our Latin American schools. This guide was not imposed upon the schools in the different countries but was presented as a service and tool for evaluation. In fact, the basic plan has such flexibility that it can serve as a guide to schools with different lengths of sessions, for day or night schools, and also makes room for studies by correspondence. A missionary was named by the missions board to serve as coordinator of the Christian education program in Latin America and to help implement the basic plan in the different schools when such help was requested.

## Advanced Leadership Training

After the basic plan had been accepted, the next need that captured the attention of the joint committee was the need for training of national leaders such as superintendents and Bible school teachers. It was quite evidently impossible for such leaders to get their training by going to the United States or some other far-removed area. The superintendents were continually occupied, as were the Bible school teachers, so that they could not afford to take leave for a whole year from their respective responsibilities. This ruled out not only the sending of students abroad, but the establishing of a school in some given point in Latin America for the training of leaders. It was recognized that to establish a regular campus and require that students attend from a distance, even though the financial problems could be solved, would certainly limit the student body to younger, unattached men; and the leaders now occupying prominent posts who needed the training would not be helped.

The solution reached by the committee was to divide all of Latin America and the West Indies into several sections with a system of month-long class sessions followed by two years of correspondence work. The plan called for three such month-long sessions and a total of four years of correspondence work. To do this, it was necessary to develop a roving faculty which could go from area to area and implement the courses of study.

Records of each student are kept in a central office, and the work done corresponds to university or seminary level. Three categories of recognition for completion of the course are granted: a certificate for those who complete the entire course satisfactorily but may not have completed all of their work as required by the basic plan for institutes; a diploma for those who complete this advanced work and have also graduated from a Bible institute; and finally, a degree for those who have received a bachelor degree for academic work, having finished also the Bible institute work and completed the advanced seminary work.

This system has proved very satisfactory at the present stage of development of the work. This is evidenced by the fact that there are over eight hundred pastors and leaders enrolled in the courses at the present time. It is, however, very demanding work for those that direct the program. The system requires much travel and long absences from home. However, the results are proving to be satisfactory, and missionaries engaged in this type of work are making an important contribution to the national churches in general. It should be noted that while at the present time the administrators of this program and most of the teachers are missionaries, the plan calls for involving an ever-increasing number of national ministers as teachers. Several such national ministers have already taught courses in the program.

One of the greatest advantages of this system is that it grew out of the conference with the national leaders themselves, and they do not feel that the program has the stamp of "Made in the U.S.A." on it. The nationals are enthusiastic supporters of this Program of Advanced Christian Education.

## *Teaching for Christian Maturity*

The next need that came into focus was the teaching of church members in the area of Christian development and maturity. In many churches the Christian teaching has largely been limited to elementary teaching given to new converts to prepare them for baptism. It was felt that pastors needed to engage in a teaching ministry that would cover the areas of Christian maturity, evangelism, and church extension. For this purpose, the elementary Bible course was developed. Originally, it contained ten small books, which were eventually combined into three volumes, with the idea that the pastor could teach his congregation a series of studies each year that might continue for three years.

This program has proved to be highly successful. In the first place, it puts materials in the hands of pastors that help them develop their teaching ministry. Second, it provides much-needed teaching for the Christians to foster their spiritual development. And third, it helps the church in its outreach because it gives training for house-to-house visitation and helps the lay preacher as he takes care of his outstation. In some countries the national church has made the teaching of this course a national project for the pastors and churches. The results have been most gratifying, and new churches have developed as a result of this activity.

Missionaries can find a most fruitful ministry by sponsoring these types of studies among the churches. One missionary engaged in this work stays the first week with the pastor to help him get started and then moves on to the next church. He has testified that it is the most satisfying ministry he has had in his years of missionary experience. The expressions of appreciation from pastors and believers are numerous. Certainly here is an area where missionaries can develop a satisfying ministry that will help the churches to become fruitful in evangelism and church development.

## Developing Church Schools

Probably the idea of Sunday Schools as we know them in the United States cannot be transferred without modification to the foreign field. Nevertheless, the operation of a church school with classes for different ages can be a very fruitful endeavor. The primary objective, of course, is the imparting of scriptural knowledge to the converts. A secondary benefit is the developing of teachers and workers as they become active in the church and assume responsibility for classes. Some have found that the church school can also become an arm for evangelism by starting branch schools in new areas with the perspective that these might develop into new churches.

The area conferences in Latin America appointed Sunday School committees with the special obligation of fostering the advancement of this type of work. The Sunday School effort joins hands with Christian education in preparing materials for lay worker training and teacher training. This effort also gives a scope of ministry for both missionaries and nationals to the church as a whole and promises to be a fruitful aspect of missionary involvement.

## Literature

Even in the main languages outside of English, evangelical literature for evangelism, Christian maturity, and ministerial development is very inadequate. Some of this is being corrected in the principal languages—Spanish, Portuguese, and French—but there is much to be done in this area.

Early in the history of the development of the work in Latin America, the need for literature was foreseen. The effort began with providing Sunday School quarterlies but developed to include tracts, paper-covered books, textbooks, etc. Here again is a ministry that is usually beyond the reach of any single national church. In Latin America there are many Spanish-speaking countries, so one publishing effort can serve them all without needlessly duplicating the effort in each country. This again provides a much-needed service to the churches, and both missionaries and nationals can find a fruitful ministry in this effort. Naturally, such a program would have to be modified as one ministers in a smaller language group. However, after the Scriptures have been translated into the language, missionaries can serve the national church by further providing needed literature.

## Evangelism

The area conferences also appointed committees on evangelism with the idea of stepping up the evangelistic activities of the established churches and initiating plans for carrying the gospel to unreached areas. The committee approved some general plans for Latin America but encouraged particularly the establishing of evangelism committees within each country that would carry out the special emphasis as might best fit the situation. Missionaries, of course, are involved in this effort in planning with the national brethren the places for campaigns and helping with the arrangements for workers, literature, etc. Sometimes missionaries themselves have been the evangelists. The missionary's ministry in evangelism is dealt with in some detail in the previous chapter, while a general plan for total evangelism is elaborated in Chapter 10, "Goals for Missions."

In this chapter we have endeavored to show how missionaries may find new avenues of service that will meet outstanding needs of the national church even though they are no longer in a pioneer church planting ministry. Such helps are normally welcomed by national leaders. Missionaries working in an area where a national church has developed should consider the pressing needs that the church faces and endeavor to find ways of meeting them.

# 9

# The Missionary's Spiritual Influence

The ministry of the missionary is essentially spiritual. This is true whether he is engaged in evangelistic work, administrative work, office work, or teaching. The national church stands in great need of a spiritual ministry that will inspire Christians and give an example to its leadership. It was pointed out in a previous chapter that a national church seldom closes its doors to a man who manifests the fruit of the Spirit and has an anointed ministry in the Word, regardless of his nationality or race.

## The Key to Success

In all that we have discussed in the previous chapters, whether it is the importance of a missionary's relationship to his fellows or his activities in missionary ministry, the key to his success in the long run will be the vitality and depth of his own spiritual life. Jesus made this point clear to His disciples before they began their world ministry when he compared himself to the True Vine and the disciples to branches and told them they were ordained to bring forth fruit (John 15:16).

This fruit included both activity and character (Galatians 5:22,23). The disciples were instructed to remain in union with the Vine in order to produce such fruit. "Apart from me you can do nothing" (John 15:5).

Missionary productivity and deep spirituality go hand in hand. It was the renowned Hudson Taylor (who dedicated his life to China) who wrote the beautiful treatise *Union and Communion*. True faith will move mountains, but how important it is for us to remain in Christ so that faith can operate through us.

Most of the problems the missionary confronts have their solution in his own spiritual life and vitality. Many problems of relationships can be traced back directly to carnal attitudes on the part of the participants.

Many obstacles before the church will yield to intercessory prayer characterized by faith. Today too little emphasis is placed on the spiritual nature of missionary work. Missionaries find their slot in the work on the field as a teacher or as an administrator, and quite often they feel that this is all that should be expected of them. But there is so much more! What about the consuming burden for those places where the name of Christ is not yet named? Where is the man who with Paul carries the problems of "all the churches"? (2 Corinthians 11:28,29). Where is the love that suffers with the weak and offended? How can we expect the national brethren to have a pastor's heart if we approach our own task with an air of professionalism and detachment?

## *The Missionary as Example*

The missionary should be an example of Christian character. The fruit of the Spirit should mature in our lives. To our shame, we must confess that there is often a great gap between our preaching and our living. We preach about the wondrous love of God but lose patience when our companions do not live up to our expectations. Quarrels develop in the missionary family that grieve the Spirit and lower the spiritual tone of the church.

In some cultures losing one's patience and speaking roughly to a friend or brother is almost an unpardonable sin. How we need to dwell in the Vine so that the fruit of righteousness and love is revealed in our lives! God grant that we, too, may be able to say, "Follow my example, as I follow the example of Christ" (1 Corinthians 11:1). Not all of us will be known as great men and not all of us will attain great ministries, but God grant that when we have finished our course on the field where God has placed us, Christian and unsaved alike will be able to say, "There was a man of God."

## The Missionary as Spiritual Leader

There is constant need for spiritual emphasis in the work of God. There is a need for the prophetic voice that calls God's people to the fulfillment of His will. Times of spiritual refreshing—outpourings of the Spirit—are needed. It is a part of the spiritual ministry of the missionary to show the way. Praying Hyde proved that it could be done in India. Jonathan Goforth led the way in China. It is said that in the time of the Korean revival, when hindrances and barriers were presented that seemed to endanger the work and the church, missionaries and nationals alike went to their knees in prayer until the obstacle was overcome and the Spirit of God could continue His work. The presence of men and women in the church who know how to pray and wage spiritual warfare spells the difference between victory and defeat.

## Leading the Church to Revival

The greatest contribution the missionary can make to the church in any country is a spiritual contribution. His ability as an administrator and organizer may be important, but it pales beside that of being a spiritual leader who is able to encourage the church and bring it into an atmosphere of revival through his teaching, praying, and the spiritual impact of his life.

God gave Solomon the key to revival for the nation of Israel in times of national distress. "When I shut up the heavens so that there is no rain, or command locusts to devour the land or send a plague among my people, if my people, who are called by my name, will humble themselves and pray and seek my face and turn from their wicked ways, then will I hear from heaven and will forgive their sin and will heal their land" (2 Chronicles 7:13,14).

Joel 2 contains the great promise of the outpouring of the Spirit, especially verse 28. Earlier in that chapter, the prophet outlines the spiritual preparation needed to bring about such blessings (Joel 2:12–17). These include repentance, humbling of self, unity among God's people, and intercession.

Charles G. Finney maintained that revival follows spiritual laws like the laws of a temporal harvest. He insisted that if we prepare the soil of the heart, God would send the rain and sunshine and give the increase that is needed.

Missionaries should see themselves primarily as channels of God's grace and blessing to the needy people to whom they minister. Jesus pointed out that even the need for workers for the ripened harvest field is to be met by spiritual means. "*Pray ye* therefore the Lord of the harvest, that He will send forth laborers into his harvest" (Matthew 9:38, KJV; emphasis added). In the final analysis the great task of world evangelism will not be accomplished by programs, as needful as these are, or by human ingenuity alone. " 'Not by might nor by power, but by my Spirit,' says the LORD Almighty" (Zechariah 4:6).

# 10

# Goals in Missions

As we acquire knowledge of the problems and needs related to our task, we should endeavor to apply it to our own situation. What is the goal for the missionary's own life and field? What should he expect to accomplish within the next five-year period?

Probably much missionary effectiveness is lost because the missionary has failed to outline for himself specific goals for his own ministry. Too many times the missionary does that which is next at hand, what seems to require his immediate attention, without planning for the accomplishment of the main objectives of his missionary effort. The missionary is pushed by circumstances, and he ends his day, his week, his year, and his term without actually having done the things he intended to do. Discipline of time is important. The missionary must learn to distinguish between pressures from circumstances and people and his obligation to fulfill his divine call. It will help to set goals and then plan the ways those goals can become realities.

For any who might question the spiritual aspect of setting goals, it should be pointed out that Moses had a goal when he led the people out of Egypt. Jesus Christ himself set a goal for the Church when He gave the commission to preach the gospel to every creature. Paul in his writings set a goal for Christian maturity.

Applying this to our present and future situation, let us set goals for spiritual maturity, for our leadership, and for evangelism.

## *The Goal of Spiritual Maturity*

How do we expect our churches on the mission field to develop within the next few years? What should our goal be for the churches as to spirituality, biblical knowledge, worship, holiness, charity, and body ministry? How can the missionary help the church attain these goals?

### *Mature Leadership*

What kind of leadership does the church need? I am sure we can agree that leadership should be progressive in the proper sense of the word. The Church needs leadership that will plan for the future and be able to adapt to the changes that come to every nation and church. Too many pastors and leaders feel they have done their part when they simply *maintain* the wheels of the work in motion, without having any definite concept of their goals. Leaders should be men of *vision* and *faith*.

Then the Church requires leadership that is unselfish. A leader who is ambitious for personal position, gain, or comfort, and who makes decisions on the basis of how these matters affect him, cannot be a true leader of the Church of Christ. A good leader, as a good shepherd, must give his life for the sheep.

Leadership should be *knowledgeable*. It is incumbent upon missionaries to find the way to help leaders develop their spiritual understanding. Leadership should not depend upon borrowed knowledge. It must be personal and experiential.

Then a leader must be *impartial*. He must realize that he is to serve the entire church and not just his friends. He must speak and act the truth even when friends do not approve.

How we can help such leadership develop cannot be answered in a simple paragraph. Actually, this is one of our lifetime tasks. Our example, our teaching, our trust in our national leaders—all play their part. Finally, of course, the national leader's own experience will have to teach him. Above all, attitudes are more important than gifts. God looks for faithful men; the ability will come later (2 Timothy 2:2). The true leader must be God's man and seek to please Christ above everything else.

## *Goal of Total Evangelism*

The purpose of a plan of evangelism is to enable us to obey the scriptural injunction to "look upon the fields," to find practical means for mobilizing the entire church in the effort of evangelism and provide a vehicle through which the Holy Spirit can work in carrying out His plan and purpose for the area.[1]

In order to put into effect a comprehensive plan for total evangelism, preparation and effort must be made on three levels: first, the missionaries; then the national leadership; and third, the pastors and their congregations. (We are addressing missionaries and place the responsibility first on them. Of course, it could be that a national leader would take the initiative in vision and inspiration.) To accomplish this, it would be well to arrange for separate meetings with the groups mentioned in order to inspire their enthusiastic support and work with them in the carrying out of the effort.

### *Motivation*

Motivation is a key to success of any combined effort. There are two spiritual sources of motivation: the Word of God and the Holy Spirit. The first step when these groups come together is to inspire the group as to the scriptural and practical nature of the plan of total evangelization. Many Scriptures show that Christ intends the whole world to hear the gospel. This includes "every creature."

The second step is to show the possibility of realizing the task. One person cannot do it alone. The solution is to *divide the task* into areas, zones, and individual churches so that each entity and finally each individual can see where he fits into the program.

Once it is shown that world evangelization is God's will and can be accomplished through the power of the Holy Spirit, the third step is to initiate a plan of action. The plan of action will begin by defining the area to be included in the effort (country, state, region).

The final step is to carry the plan of action to every level of the church, beginning with the national executives and then into the sectional areas and to the pastors.

Such a plan can logically be divided into two areas. The first area will be what can be reached by the activity of the local churches. If a church is in a large city, the local church will find much room for activity in the city itself. Churches in smaller towns can decide which neighboring towns they will enter or in which communities they will establish outstations and branch churches.

The second area of concern will be the responsibility of the executives together with the missionaries. This has to do with establishing new churches in towns or cities where no church is established as a starter.

### Providing for Total Evangelism

The planning must include, first of all, the *workers*. This may include the securing of evangelists, whether from outside the country or from the national churches and organization.

The second concern perhaps will be the providing of proper *tools for evangelism*. This will include literature to back up the evangelistic outreach. Also included will be plans for the use of radio and the setting up of campaigns in strategic areas.

The *financial aspect* of the outreach will have to be considered and a practical plan evolved. Local churches should be included in the financial plan of total evangelism.

It should be remembered that it is not enough to outline a plan. For the plan to be successful, there must be provision for following through. National executives and missionaries must take the project on their hearts and give encouragement, advice, and prayer support to the effort. It may be advisable for the national executives to designate a special period of time for the churches to concentrate on these efforts. For example, a certain goal may be announced for a given year in which each church should mother a new church. Some national churches have designated a specific year "The Year of Total Evangelism" for their country.

### The Local Assembly

One of the most vital aspects of the plan of total evangelism is the mobilization of the local assembly to carry out the work of evangelizing their immediate community and surrounding areas.

In order for the local church to carry on an aggressive evangelism program, workers need to be prepared in two areas: first, the local worker, who will preach in the outstations and attempt to develop branch churches; then the total membership, which should be encouraged to engage in personal evangelism and saturation evangelism in a house-to-house ministry. All levels of workers should be gathered for workers' weekly prayer meetings and study. This should be carried out on both the local and regional levels, although the regional level may have to limit such meetings to once a month. In this meeting, reports will be presented and there should be an exchange of ideas and experiences as to methods employed. Naturally, this type of activity prepares the heart for periods of fervent prayer, which brings the blessings of God upon the church and the activities of the individual members.

## *Planning for Reaching Goals*

We are now thinking of individual missionary goals to be established in relation to a particular country.

The missionary should earnestly seek God to find out his part in reaching the goal of total evangelism. This is more than an intellectual exercise. Should he change his location? Could God be calling him to devote more time to evangelism?

The missionary can also use his influence with the leadership of the national organization. The national executives need to see that it is their responsibility not only to take care of the churches that already exist but to do some positive planning for the "regions beyond." Here is another area of contribution the missionary can make to evangelism, through instructing and stimulating the national church to become effective in its outreach.

It is important that the missionary not simply draw up plans himself and then expect the national brethren to come along. Rather, he should share his burden with the brethren; but in the actual working of the plans, he would do well to let the ideas come from the national brethren themselves with perhaps an occasional suggestion and stimulation from his own thinking. It is in this type of planning that the true partnership with the national church evolves.

One question he could well explore with the national brethren is whether a mission could be established. What about reaching an indigenous tribe? When will the national church establish a missions department so that the local churches become a part of the worldwide outreach of the church?

Other questions to be considered are the following: What *evangelistic campaigns* have been conducted in the country under consideration? What more can be done? Where are the strategic cities in which campaigns should be held? Has adequate follow-up been implemented? Have new churches been established as a result of these efforts?

Today's world calls for decisive missionary action. The opportunities to make a meaningful contribution to world evangelism have never been greater. In establishing goals for his personal ministry, the missionary should not simply depend upon human reasoning or "pick his goals out of the air," but rather he should see himself as a channel for the fulfilling of the divine purpose of God in world evangelism. This means that the missionary must be a man led and inspired by the Spirit of God. The Holy Spirit will lead him in such a way that plans made will fit the culture and the people and will bring about the greatest success possible.

What a challenge faces the missionary today! He lives in a strategic period in the history of the world and of the Church. He is called of God to carry out God's purposes in today's world. He has a clear mandate from the Scriptures, and divine guidance is open to him if he will but bring his own life in tune with the divine program.

We see great things ahead. With the national church carrying the administration of the work, the missionary can be freed from the obligations of such details. He can devote more time to prayer, Bible study, and evangelism. He can return once again to the true missionary ministry, which is a spiritual contribution to plant, establish, expand, and strengthen the Church in the land of his calling.

## Endnote

[1] Some of the main steps in this plan for Total Evangelism are taken from "A Practical Plan for Total Evangelism," a paper which grew out of a meeting of national executives and missionaries of the AG in Central America in Matagalpa, Nicaragua, and was assigned to missionary Ralph D. Williams for proper elaboration.